Angela —
May this book
encourage you as you
read it. Whatever your
your purpose is greater

MY
PAIN
HAD
Purpose

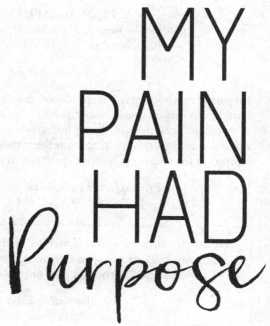

MY PAIN HAD *Purpose*

Marked for Death, Yet I Live

YVETTE STEELE

purposely created PUBLISHING

MY PAIN HAD PURPOSE
Published by Purposely Created Publishing Group™
Copyright © 2017 Yvette Steele

Printed in the United States of America
ISBN: 978-1-945558-87-0

Special discounts are available on bulk quantity purchases by book clubs, associations and special interest groups. For details email: sales@publishyourgift.com or call (888) 949-6228.

For information logon to:
www.PublishYourGift.com

Dedication

This book is dedicated to those who are struggling to find their purpose; to those who are still in bondage and feel that, because of their past, God cannot use them; to those who are still carrying the shame, hurt, and pain from being violated, abandoned, neglected, and abused. Yes, those things did happen, but they now have permission to be set free.

"So if the Son sets you free, you will be free indeed."
—John 8:36 NIV

Table of Contents

Acknowledgments

To God, who is my everything. It takes an awesome God to forgive and redeem a stained individual like me and turn my pain into purpose, then use me for His glory, allowing me to share my journey to bless others.

To my husband, Emerson V. Steele: Thank you for supporting me in the ministry that God has assigned to me and your humbleness to allow your own redemption to be shared in this book. Thank you for recognizing the mask I was wearing and for giving me the strength and courage to remove it. I honor and respect you for your strength, love, and commitment for our family, and your humbleness and submission to God. You are indeed my Boaz.

To my four wonderful children, Shante', Pierre, Brandon, and Steven: It is truly a blessing and an honor to be your mother. You bring me so much joy and I am so proud of the accomplishments that you have made and are still obtaining in your lives. You are indeed blessed. I truly believe that you were predestined to be my offspring and God gave us to each other. For this, I am so grateful. Thank you for always supporting me and for sharing me with those who God places in my path to encourage.

To my parents, Joseph and Lucile Brown Jr.: Words cannot express my gratitude and love for the both of you. Thank you, Mommy, for the many sacrifices you made for me, for opening your big heart to take a little baby girl and shower her with comfort and love. I thank both of you for your support, forgiveness, guidance, discipline, and love. You've not only shown and exposed me to so many wonderful things, but you have also done the same for your grandchildren and this is something that we will always treasure.

To my sister, Courtni Jo-L Edwards Brown Weathers: I thank you for being a wonderful aunt, my biggest cheerleader, friend, and confidant. You've allowed me to share many joyful and painful things with you while always leaving me with words of encouragement and reminding me that you have my back. We share a bond like no other.

Evangelist, First Lady, Prophetess Joanna B. Coles, my spiritual mother: There is not a day that goes by that I do not thank God for that faithful day He brought you into my life. Your outpouring of wisdom, prayers, counsel, love, and guidance have truly been a blessing to me. Thank you for your support and encouragement, especially during those difficult times while writing this book exposed the areas of my life that weren't completely healed. You are a gift to me from God.

To Bishop and the late Pastor MacKall: You were that ram in the bush. I will forever be thankful to you both; because of you, I began to turn back to God and accept the calling and assignments on my life. Thank you for ministering to me, taking me under your tutelage, and for your many days and hours of laboring with me at the altar. This became the spiritual turning point in my life.

Lastly, to my great-grandparents, the late Bishop Arthur R. Christian and Lillian Christian: If it had not been for you anointing my head and praying over me at such a young age, where would I be? I'm thankful to you for living all you knew how for the Lord and for being that godly example that a little girl could see and remember for all her days. To be absent from the body is to be present with the Lord and your labor was not in vain.

Foreword

"You should greatly rejoice in what is waiting for you, even if now for a little while you have to suffer various trials. Suffering tests your faith which is more valuable than gold (remember that gold, although it is perishable, is tested by fire) so that if it is found genuine, you can receive praise, honor, and glory when Jesus the Anointed, our Liberating King, is revealed at last."

—Peter 1:6-7

Diamonds are formed under extreme heat and unfounded torque. Gold also requires intense temperatures in order to be refined and produce the purest twenty-four karats. Life has a way of creating extreme situations; some are beyond our wildest imagination.

Two years ago, while ministering at a women's retreat, I met a beautiful woman with a heart of gold, as resilient as a diamond. After spending time with her, I realized that her natural, statuesque grace and beauty were a complete contrast to her past; her elegance was not a façade to cover all the unnatural pain she had endured, but a genuine residual result of the perpetual hand of God in and on her life. Deep within her were dreams, talents, and gifts waiting to be birthed. She had experienced trauma and tragedy, but walked triumphantly. She was victimized, but came out a victor. Her story had to be told. *My Pain Had Purpose* is Yvette Steele's story.

This intriguing project will pull you into the world of a woman who endured unthinkable and unfathomable mental, physical, and emotional pain, heartache, and abuse. On this tumultuous journey, you will witness her potent yet futile acts of revenge, her folly of trying to do things on her own, her fear when her life was threatened, and her faith that continues to resolve her issues.

This provocative work will not only uplift and bless you, but it will seep into your aged wounds and release a balm of healing and deliverance. It will lovingly nudge you to take an introspective glimpse of your relationship with the Lord and make the necessary adjustments. This book will help you to forgive, move forward, and discover the purpose in your own pain.

Authored by one individual, this impactful composition will resonate with and be relevant to so many. Prepare your heart to embrace this invaluable treasure. Experience the formation of a jewel. Read it. Re-read it, again and again. Share it and let it bless you down to your toes. There *is* purpose in pain, but most all of there is purpose in *you*.

Providentially purposeful and intentional,
Evangelist Joanna B. Coles
First Lady, Jurisdiction Three
The Convention of Covenanting Churches
Lorton, Virginia

Introduction

"And they have conquered him by the blood of the Lamb and by the word of their testimony, for they loved not their lives even unto death."

—Revelation 12: 11(ESV)

I often listen to individuals give their testimonies of past trials, of how they were raped, did drugs, or were molested; and then they'd share how their Lord and Savior Jesus Christ delivered and brought them out. Each time, the congregation would erupt in praise and worship for what God had done in their lives. But, how do you stand and give a testimony about multiple traumas you've faced in life?

How do I stand up in front of a congregation that sees me as being put together from head-to-toe and always becoming of a lady, and share with them that I had been molested, been physically and mentally abused, been raped, attempted suicide, had an abortion, had miscarriages, and more? How do I avoid being judged, being looked at differently, or tarnishing the image my family always wanted to maintain? How do

I express that, throughout my life, I've asked, "Lord, where do I belong? Why me and why don't I fit in? Am I not good enough?" How do I talk about or ask these things when I am still trying to remember some of my own childhood memories, not knowing if it I had blocked them from my remembrance or if the Lord is shielding me from them? We are often taught to "keep family business in the family" or never to discuss what happens inside your home; the only problem is that many of us never get the help we need.

Can you imagine being a child who grew up in two completely different places, having to keep secrets and adjusting your personality to adapt to whichever environment you were in at that time? Walking around with so much pain and fear, being threatened that, if you told anyone about the things being done to you, you'd be forbidden from ever going to the one place that brings you some joy and happiness? Can you imagine facing one of the scariest things in your life, and instead of receiving help, being sent away like trash? Or wearing a mask most of your life to hide your pain and living with a wall up for so long that you end up not even knowing who you are?

How can I tell these people that I'm running from my calling?

Thinking about all this, my answer was no: I could not stand up and share my truth, my story, my testimony with anyone—that is until now.

Today, you are not reading about a victim, but a survivor and an overcomer. Understanding that the enemy had marked me for death from the moment I was conceived, I have been compelled to share my testimony with the world. I pray this book encourages you not to give up and, instead, to hold on to God. Hold on to His unchanging hand, never letting go, and know that He will never leave nor forsake you. He will be there even during your midnight hour, for He is a healer and a deliverer.

God is on your side.

CHAPTER ONE

■

An Awakening

"But I will call on God, and the lord will rescue me.
Morning, noon, and night I cry out in my distress,
and the lord hears my voice."
—Psalms 55:16-17 (NLT)

One bright and glorious morning, I was awakened by the sound of the birds chirping outside. They were extremely loud for some reason this day, and the sun was so bright, it pierced through the blinds of my bedroom windows. My son was still sleeping; my husband had left already. Fall was still in the air. Why was I feeling so strange? I couldn't even push myself out of the bed, and out of nowhere, I started to cry uncontrollably. What was this piercing pain that I was feeling? A pain so deep and overwhelming that it could only come from my heart and soul. All I could do was ask the Lord to help me. Whatever this was, I knew I had to get myself together.

I had just experienced a kind of hurt like no other. My husband, my protector, the man I adored, loved with everything in me, and prayed for every day; the man I had the upmost respect for, the head of our home; the man I removed my mask and tore down my wall for; the only one I'd ever shared my complete life story with—he was unfaithful to me. He'd been disrespectful towards me, allowed others to disrespect me, hung out with the wrong people, and lied to me. The Christ I saw in him was fading, and no longer was I or Christ first in his life. Without my protective barriers, I was unable to suppress my feelings or bring them under control. I had no choice but to feel out the hurt, pain, disappointment and brokenness.

As I forced myself out of the bed, I hit the floor unable to stand. My legs felt like they had become noodles. It seemed that every disappointment, abandonment, abuse, hurt, and disrespectful thing I had buried had risen to the surface, and all I could do was drag myself on the floor, crying until I couldn't move anymore. It was then that I realized that I was completely broken by the things that I'd endured in my life, and the mask I was so used to having up to protect me from these emotions were no longer there. I laid there on the floor for what seemed liked hours, crying out to the Lord, releasing to Him everything that happened to me, along with everyone who did me wrong and caused me hurt, including the hurt I caused to myself.

I realized that I was no longer living life and had allowed myself to get caught up in the cycle of just going through the motions of each day. I was taking care of others, putting them first and making sure they were happy, all at the expense of myself. I was putting up a front to protect the reputation of those I loved, all while trying to stay true to who I thought I was. But this was no longer possible. Finally, I came face-to-face with the realization that this had become a pattern in my life: Trying to be the best mother, wife, sister, daughter, and friend a woman can be. Unfortunately, this was too stressful and unattainable.

My number one desire had always been to make sure that others were encouraged, comfortable, happy, and pleased with my decisions, even though, at times, I was bound to fail. Whatever I said or did was based on what they wanted and expected from me. It was my need to feel wanted, to fit in, to be loved and accepted. Feeling and living like this lead to many bad decisions such as looking constantly for love, entering bad relationships, not fulfilling my dreams, evading my troubles, and ultimately running from my calling and the church.

It was at that moment laying on my floor, in the bedroom I shared with my husband amid my brokenness, the Lord took me on a journey—a journey to reveal to me all that I'd dealt with. Because I was always putting others before myself, I was slowly allowing the enemy to kill me, naturally and spiritually. Calling my name ever so softly, the Lord let me know that it was time for me to surrender, to let it go, to heal and receive total deliverance. A time for complete restoration. I needed to know who Yvette was, the unique human being He created and cannot ever be duplicated, and to know my purpose in life.

This journey required me not only to remember the good times, but also to face those dark memories I had suppressed for many years. They played a critical role in the things I accepted, how I viewed myself, and how I made future decisions that ultimately affected my life on many levels. Surrendering, I was ready to face my truth, look back at my journey, and allow total healing and restoration to take place.

He began by showing me that, I had to first practice with self-forgiveness, absolving myself for accepting blame for the actions taken against me by others and for putting up an emotional wall that, instead of protecting me, caused me more harm than good. Also, I needed to forgive myself for not listening and being obedient to the voice of the Lord and His instructions for my life that were meant to confront the real issues that were affecting me.

There is a difference between happiness and joy: The world gives me happiness, depending on belongings and circumstances, but only God can give me His joy. I realized that I deserved to be truly filled with His unwavering triumph and wanted to experience all that He had for me. I now wanted Him to use me for His glory and to have an obedient spirit to do all that He would call me to do, with authority and power.

I no longer wanted to accept anything less, but instead, walk in the kingdom authority that God had given me.

As I lay still on the floor, Jesus wrapped His loving arms around me. I began to feel peace and comfort, hearing His sweet voice whispering in my ear, "You are not alone. I will never leave you."

CHAPTER TWO

■

The Beginning

"Before I formed you in the womb I knew you, and before you were born I consecrated you; I appointed you a prophet to the nations."
— **Jeremiah 1:5 (ESV)**

Giving birth to a child is an exciting time for most. It's a time to celebrate, bring families together, and rejoice in a gift and blessing from God. But this is not always the case. Some are faced with bringing life into an already struggling situation or one without support from the other parent. Some are forced into parenthood due to religious beliefs, while others deal with an existing abusive relationship. However, the one thing many forget is how these things affect the child who is soon to enter the world.

The day had come for the arrival of a bouncing, beautiful little girl with full hair, the seventh one out of ten children.

Yes, she was truly a blessing from God, preordained to make her arrival on this specific day at this specific time. Already known by Christ, appointed, anointed, and called before she was even formed in her mother's womb, she, like so many others before her, was brimming with unlimited possibilities. She was unaware of the pain she would endure or the reasons behind them. This little baby girl was me.

The earliest memory I can recall is around the age of five-years-old. I'm still unsure why I can't remember anything before that or some things in between. One clear thing I remember is not being around my natural siblings all the time and being the only one transported back and forth between what seemed like two completely different environments. Often, I wondered why none of the other siblings I saw and played with came with me, even to places like the circus and dance classes. I would later learn that an arrangement had been made so that my uncle (who was the younger brother of my birth mother) and my aunt (his wife at the time) could help raise me, since my birth father, who is also the father of the previous six children, had abandoned my birth mother, leaving her to raise seven children alone. This would later explain why the other children never came with me, since I was the only child these arraignments had been made for. The day would also come when I would learn that my aunt whom I thought had given birth to me, who also provided an environment filled with love, happiness, protection and comfort, and the only woman I called "mommy" and "mother" was not actually my biological mother. Instead, the woman I would go visit and stay with from time to time in an environment that brought me fear and sadness, was the woman who gave birth to me.

Having to live in two different environments caused many nights of crying myself to sleep, wondering why no one wanted to keep me full-time, what was wrong with me, and what did I do wrong that caused to have to live in two different families. All the while, I also had to deal with my natural siblings holding resentment towards me for this arrangement, a decision I had nothing to do with. They would often say things to me like "You think you are better than us," "Don't forget, we are your real family," or "Have you forgotten where you came from?" Of course, I couldn't understand why they felt those things, because none of it was what I actually thought. Despite me constantly trying to prove that I loved and cared about them, we would end up going through years of ups and downs with our relationship. This eventually caused me to start doubting and questioning God's love: Why would He allow me to live in a world that was often filled with beautiful things, love, and joy; then send me to one surrounded by violence, poverty, crime, anger, and pain?

This type of situation would be difficult on any person, so imagine a child having to grow up living like this. There were times when I would wake up in circumstances that every child would dream to be in: The only child with a beautiful room filled with toys, showered with so much love, dressed in the prettiest clothes (sometimes matching my mother's), and taken to explore some fascinating places. I was protected from anything that caused me harm. But, these pleasures always reminded me that I had to go back to an environment where I could play with the other children, but I was not the only child, had to share a bedroom, sometimes a bed, and often felt out of place, lonely, scared, and unwelcomed.

I received constant verbal and physical abuse in that latter world. I never knew if the belt, the iron, the shoe, the hand, a broomstick, extension cord, or all would strike me at any moment, often with my not knowing the reason for my punishment. I could not call my aunt "mommy" in the presence of my natural siblings or in the presence of my birth mother because, if I did, everyone would attack me with vicious and hurtful words. Yet, my birth mother would not allow my natural siblings or myself to call her "mommy." We all had to call her by her first name as if she didn't want people to know she had so many children. My aunt was the only person I recognized, as my mother and called "mommy," and yet, it became almost forbidden to even talk about her let alone mention her name, for it would result in me receiving some type of physical punishment. Why would someone be so angry towards an individual that is supposed to be a blessing to you? I still do not understand to this day.

Not only were my worlds different when it came to my family atmosphere, but they were different spiritually. I was shuffled between a traditional Baptist church and a strict Pentecostal-Apostolic church; thus, I sat under two different ways of preaching and teaching. This was the beginning of me learning God. The only thing the two churches had in common was that neither allowed women preachers.

I remember crying myself to sleep when I knew it was time for me to make that journey to my birth mother's house, often crying the entire trip and reaching out, hoping my mother would not make me go, for I never knew what awaited me there. My only comfort when I had to go back there were the times my great-grandparent's, whom we affectionately called Poppa and Nanny, would be present. My birth mother had lived in the home before her many moves over the next few years. Though extremely strict, my great-grandparents were God-fearing people and I always felt safe when they were present.

Often hearing prayers coming from my great-grandparent's bedroom, I would sneak and stand near the door so that I could hear them clearer, while thinking to myself, "She sure does pray a lot. Why does she have so much to tell God?" From time to time, I would hear her mention my name along with other family members, so, of course, I thought we must be in trouble, because they would always sing in church, "You can just call on Jesus, and tell him all about your troubles." So, while quietly standing outside their door, I would softly start praying, telling the Lord I was sorry and did not want to be in trouble.

My great-grandfather wore wired, round-rim glasses, a cozy sweater, and his clergy shirt with the white collar, and he carried his Bible with him, ready to counsel those who would come to the house troubled. Always hearing him talk about the God he served and how good He was, prompted me to start asking my great-grandmother questions about God.

There were times when my great-grandmother would put this oil on my forehead and start to pray over me. She would call me and say, "Vette, come here and let me pray over you." Though I did not know anything about anointing oil and was unsure if anyone else in the house was having this done, I went gleefully. At the time, I thought she was putting used cooking grease on my forehead. One thing I knew for sure was that I liked when she did it because it made me feel safe and I treasured those special moments with her.

My great-grandparent's home was a place that held a lot of memories: My ears getting pierced with a stick needle that was put to the fire first, then to my earlobe, creating a hole that they quickly inserted a piece of broom straw through to keep it from closing. The smell of burnt hair in the kitchen from the women getting their hair straightened and curled for Sunday morning church the next day. Everyone knew if you lived in that house, you had to get up and go to Holy Trinity Apostolic Church on Sunday.

I was excited when it was time to go to my great-grand-parent's church on those Sunday mornings. With the other children, I patiently waited for service to end, smelling the chicken being fried and the biscuit being baked in the sanctuary. We would run upstairs to the banquet hall after the first service, have dinner, then go outside and play until the evening service. And, when the older kids were nice to us, they would let us go to the candy store with them.

Sitting in church, my eyes were always fixated on my great-grandfather, Bishop Christian, as they would call him, standing in the pulpit declaring the Word of God, sweating and heaving and giving all he had to preaching. All the while, my great-grandmother would be sitting on the front pew, dressed in all-white from head to toe, praying aloud at times, calling on the name of Jesus, watching everything that was happening in the church. We knew better not to move or even get up to use the bathroom unless it was an emergency.

I would be looking around, saying to myself, "Lord, what is happening in here?" Seeing how the people in there were dancing and singing and speaking in ways I didn't understand, yet feeling safe at the same time was strange to me. This never happened in the Baptist church my mother took me to. They were always so quiet and barely even raised their hands or said "Hallelujah," and, if by chance someone did, they would quickly get a strange look.

Now, at my great-grandparents' church men and ladies would fall out on the floor and then others would come and cover them with a white sheet. At first, I would be scared, wondering if they had all died. But then, they would rise and begin to shout and dance, thanking God, speaking in a strange language I couldn't understand. It was a feeling I could not explain, but one I would never forget—whenever I walked into any church, I looked for that same feeling. I would tell my friends at church, "I'm going to speak that strange language, dance, and fall out like them when I get older." They would look at me and laugh. Of course, now I understand that, what I thought was a strange feeling and strange behavior back then, was the presence, anointing, and movement of the Spirit of God in the church.

Singing in the children's choir and being in Sunday school were fun times for me. I just didn't understand at the time why we had to be in church all day. There was one event that took place for which I still do not understand the purpose. I had to be the bride in a kiddy mock wedding, known as a "Tom Thumb Wedding." These weddings are named for Tom Thumb, a dwarf in P. T. Barnum's circus, who married another dwarf named Lavinia Warren in an elaborate ceremony in Manhattan in 1863. Many churches did these as a way of fundraising. I would walk down the aisle in the church with this mini-wedding dress and veil on, carrying flowers, peaking, and seeing my wedding party who were children my age, standing at the altar before a church full of people.

I was scared, thinking, "I know I'm too young to be getting married. I'm just a little girl." So, I pretended that I was marrying Jesus since He didn't have a wife, based on what we had learned in Sunday school. Looking back now, it may have been at that very moment I knew I belonged to Christ without realizing it. We even had a mini preacher. He was around my age and played with me outside in between services. I'm not sure how much money the church raised from those weddings, but as far as I knew, I married Jesus so He would not be alone.

Knowing that my great-grandparents' home was a place of safety for me brought me comfort; if I was there, I would be okay. There was one incident that, if it hadn't been for my Nanny, the outcome would have been far worst. It's something I hid and carried around with me all my life. Although he apologized to me when I was twenty-years-old, I still never told anyone about it, even after having my own children until a few years ago.

I could hear my great-grandmother's voice calling for me in the distance, but I could not answer her because I was being held down with hands over my mouth. I was being threatened not to say a word. It was my brother. He forced my panties down around my ankles and begin to penetrate me. But, my great-grandmother would not stop calling my name until I answered her; he had no choice but to remove his hands. Yelling out to her that I was coming, he released and allowed me to get up, but not before threatening me that he would harm me if I told anyone, and saying no one would believe me anyway.

This was the beginning of sexual abuse and assault in my life. The next time, another family member would force my hands to touch his genitals. It was also the beginning of me learning to hide my emotions and feelings. Having just experienced something so traumatic and unable to fully comprehend what and why this was done to me, I dared not tell anyone, out of fear of being hurt and blamed. I was frightened of my brothers: I had always been taught that, if a person goes to jail, it was because they had done something extremely bad, and knowing my brothers were always in some type of trouble, I remained quiet. Therefore, I allowed this to become one of the many painful secrets and burdens I would carry in life. This also was the beginning of me blaming myself for the pain that others caused me.

One day, I was going through an old photo album of my mother's and saw several photos of me as a small child with my mother and I celebrating various holidays. Pictures of us in the kitchen, dressed alike in our leather or fur coats, places we visited, and more. I looked so happy in the photos; there were even a few photos in the book showing me with a tall, handsome man during my earlier years. Pictures of him holding me up in the air and me looking so excited and happy, but not so many other photos of him after that.

I eventually was made aware the man in the pictures was my biological uncle. He and my mommy were only married for a few years which explained why I had no memory of him being a constant presence in my life, and looking back, I can see my life as I knew changed when they divorced. I found myself spending more time with my birth mother and siblings. However, upon looking through the photos I also noticed I was unable to find any photos of me with my birth mother or birthfather. I did, though, come across a photo of me in a metal crib in a hospital, which brought back memories of that experience.

Children's Hospital in Washington DC is a huge and scary place to a child, especially one who is six years old and has to stay for a procedure. I had knots on my head. The doctors shaved my head completely so they could cut open the knots and drain the fluid that had built up in them to prevent infection from setting in and possibly spreading. The scars from that procedure are still visible to this day on my scalp. I woke to my entire head wrapped like a mummy lying in a huge metal bed. I can remember my mother coming to the hospital, bringing me paper dolls to play with and treats to comfort me, but I cannot recall my birth mother visiting or bringing me anything for comfort. Later, I was told the knots formed from my hair being pulled too tight by my birth mother, which caused pus and fluid to form as knots. I believe this was the first attempt of the enemy to take my life—but God.

After being released, I was now a child walking around with a bald head. Still a little girl, I thought nothing of it—that is until I started getting teased. My mother would put the cutest and most stylist hats on my head to match my outfits while telling me I was such a pretty little girl. But, I remember my birth mother making me wear this curly wig, as if she was ashamed to let anyone see my head bald. Of course, my siblings, along with other family members, would tease me and call me names, sometimes snatching the wig off and tossing it between them. Yes, this may be normal behavior of kids poking fun, but when you are already being mistreated and feeling as though you are not wanted, it just adds to the emotional damage and low self-esteem.

When I went to my birth mother to complain, I would receive the same angry response to anything I told or asked her: "Get out of my face with that foolishness before I smack you and stop acting like you think you are better than them. I'm the one who gave birth to you, I'll take you away, and never let you go over there again." With this kind of threat being constant, I began to genuinely believe that she would keep me from my mother, especially since my birth mother seemed to have such a distain for her. So, I learned to hold everything in and act like everything was okay.

When my great-grandparents were around, my birth mother never cursed at us or was physically abusive. Not that we never got spanked, but being disciplined for something and being abusive are two different things. This was the beginning of me recognizing that my siblings did not have a problem walking all over me and that I was the outsider. Often, when something was done and somebody was going to get in trouble, they quickly blamed it on me without hesitation or add me to the list, even if I was never involved. During one incident, one of my sisters and I were locked in the basement as punishment, which was a dark and cold place. You'd have to go down a long stairway that leads into darkness and pull a string at the bottom step to turn on the lights. We both were punished when it was only one of us that should have been. I sat at the top steps by the door, crying, while she was down in the basement, riding a bike, laughing about lying on me. In those moments, I just wanted my mother to come rescue me or the God my great-grandfather spoke about to come help me.

When my mother would pack my suitcase for me to return to my birth mother's, she always gave me a little allowance for the chores I did. After waking up many times to find my money missing, I had to start sleeping with it safety-pinned to the inside of my pajamas. This made me mad and sad because I didn't mind sharing or treating my siblings to things, if only they asked. I learned quickly that I had to protect what was mine or it would be taken from me.

In my suitcase, my mother always folded my clothes neatly and arranged them by outfits, from hair bows and undergarments to socks and shoes, so that all I had to do was lift that outfit and get dressed. The only problem was that there would be times when one of my sisters would wear my clothing before I had an opportunity to. Of course, when I complained to my birth mother, I would somehow end up in trouble, which often left me wearing dirty, worn undergarments and clothing, because I only had enough outfits for each day. For fear of getting hit or punished, there was so much I never told my birth mother. Unfortunately, that didn't stop the verbal or physical abuse. The hardest part was pretending around people that everything was okay; you never knew when her hand would go flying to hit you in your face.

As the years moved on, my great-grandparents went on to glory, and I no longer had them to protect me. I now had to go stay wherever my birth mother was living, which changed often. We'd be in an apartment in the projects in Southeast Washington, DC off Stanton Road, where crime and shootings took place constantly; then, six months later we'd be living in upper Northwest DC where she'd rent a house. Once, when living in an apartment on the Southeast side, my birth mother sent me downstairs to get the mail, and I heard something that sounded like a firecracker. I turned to see a man running up the stairs with a gun in his hand. He paused for a moment and looked right at me; unable to move, I just looked back at him. For whatever reason, he turned away and ran out the door. I looked around to see if he saw someone, but there was no one there. In retrospect, that was another moment, the second attempt when the enemy wanted to take me out—but God.

It was during these times that I have the earliest memory of truly crying out to God.

"Lord! Oh, Lord! What have I done? Am I a bad child who no one wants to keep full-time? Why must I go back and forth between these two worlds? Does my mother not see me kicking, screaming, and crying while holding on to her, begging her not to leave me? Does she know I'm constantly being threatened? Oh, Lord, my birth mother causes me so much pain—she acts like she hates me and looks at me as if she despises me."

Different men came in and out of my birth mother's life: many of whom were not kind to her, none of whom she ever married, yet were often treated better by her than us. We were told to accept and respect them, and to call them "Uncle" or "Mister." One morning, while living in one of the many places my birth mother moved into, I smelled bacon and eggs being prepared. I was excited because I thought, "Wow, we are going to have a good breakfast this morning." I happily hurried myself downstairs only to find a man sitting at the table, eating the delicious food I was smelling. Watching her serve him and making sure he had everything he needed to enjoy his meal, I sat patiently ready for mine. Well, that's not what I got. Instead, I was told, "What's wrong with you? Get your behind up and put some oatmeal in a bowl from the pot on the stove."

Wondering why I could not have bacon and eggs too, I asked. That was the wrong thing to say and the last thing I remember before her fist came swinging back and hit me so hard I fell out of the chair. Blood seeped from where my teeth bit down on my bottom lip. I sat up, mostly confused, because I just got knocked to the floor by the woman who gave birth to me, just for saying that I wanted to eat the same food she was serving this man sitting across me. This was the same man who, at times, was abusive to her and always wanted me to sit on his lap, and when I didn't, I was yelled at. The reason I never wanted to sit on his lap was because I would feel his private part pulsating on me, and I had the fear that he would try to do to me the same thing my brother had done early on. But, of course, I could never tell my birth mother what was happening; she always believed him over us anyway.

It seemed like the anger and abuse were getting worse. There were times my birth mother would be gone and my siblings' activities would lead to something breaking in the house. This one day was no different and, like many times before, they decided they were going to tell her that I had done it. The fear of her coming back and beating me with one of the many objects of her choice overwhelmed me; I decided that day I was going to run away. I was going to run to my mother's parents who lived by Howard University. Once I ran out the house, it dawned on me that where she lived seemed so far away, and I was not quite sure of the quickest way to get there. Of course, it was not that far at all, but to a child, it was.

I ran out of the house and went around to the corner to use the payphone in front of the neighborhood store so that I could call my mother to come get me, but it was broken. Not sure what to do next, I just stood there, crying and scared, often having passerby's stop to ask if I was okay or lost. Soon after, two of my siblings came around the corner looking for me, talking me back into coming to the house, promising me that our birth mother was not going to beat me, especially since I didn't do anything. Well, once again, that was a lie and I was beaten, left with whip marks and threats while they laughed. This is not to say I never did any wrong or my siblings weren't hit—they had their share of beatings and unjust punishments as well. However, being that I was not around all the time seemed to play a heavier part as to why I was singled out, not just by her, but also by them.

Most people sharing their story would tell you about physical fights they had at school, but who knew I would end up having one with my own biological sister? Although I was masking and suppressing the emotions, they were building up and, at some point, they needed to come out. That moment came one day when my sister kept bullying me and I had had enough. Standing near the steps leading from the back door, she pushed me and all the anger from years of being bullied, teased, lied on and more rose to the surface, and I lost it—I hit her and knocked her down the steps. I no longer felt afraid of her, but the moment also scared me because I wanted to kill her. That anger and rage was something I had never felt before. Once again, my birth mother accused me of this incident, punishing me for thinking I was better than my sister.

I wanted to know at what point any of this— the threats, the beatings, the non-showing of love, the belittling, and more—was going to stop. The only time my birth mother showed any type of joy and excitement was when I marched down the street in a parade as a majorette with the band. Did this woman not like me because of what my biological father had done to her? Was I being punished for the actions of a man I did not even know or never even met? I wondered this until one day, at the age of ten, I was taken to the projects to meet his mother.

In a crowded room, people sat around, laughing and talking loudly. Being guided over to this older woman sitting in a chair, I was asked if I knew who she was; of course, my nervous answer was no. All at once, multiple people were saying, "That's your grandmother, child!" As I stood there, quietly thinking, "She is not my grandmother. I don't know her," I heard someone yell, "Well, don't stand there. Say hi and give her a hug." So, I slowly bent down to give her a hug and said how nice it was to meet her.

I soon noticed that several of the people in the room looked like my older siblings and even me. Then, a woman came up to grab my hand and said, "Come on so you can meet your family. You look just like your daddy, sweetie pie."

I stopped and asked who sweetie pie was, because I thought my birthfather's name was Richard. The room then erupted in laughter. The woman told me that "sweetie-pie" was a nickname for my birthfather, and she was my aunt, one of his sisters.

While making our way around to meet everyone, I saw a man in the distance who looked amazingly like me. As we made our way up to him, the woman asked him, "Sweet-pie, do you know who this is?" He slowly raised his head, looking directly at me and said, "No!"

"This is your youngest child."

I quickly turned my head and asked, "This is my birthfather?"

I turned back to look at him, waiting for him to say something. I'm not sure what I was expecting—maybe a hug or him asking how I was—but I knew for sure that his response was not what I wanted: All he said was, "Oh really. Wow." With that, I became angry. "Well nice to meet you too," I said, snatching my hand out of hers and walking away. That was the last time I'd see him until the day of his funeral.

Here I was: One parent didn't know who I was and one acted like she hated me, and I was still unable to share any of this with by mother for fear of not being able to see her again. Crying in the midnight hours, asking the Lord what kind of life I was living, became normal for me. I learned to prepare myself to endure the pain and disappointments.

As years went on, things became unbearable for me. I felt trapped for not being able to tell anyone what was happening to me, so I decided that I was going to try one last time to pray and cry out to the lord. I told Him everything, just in case He did not know or missed something. I was going to ask Him all the questions I needed answers to while lying in my bed at my mother's. I started asking Him, "How do I fix this Lord? How do I escape this? Why so much pain? Why me? Why is my birth mother abusive towards me? Why can't I live in one place permanently? Why did you let her give birth to me? Why don't I fit in anywhere? How do I handle my sisters and brothers who look at me as an outsider? Why doesn't my mother want to keep me full-time? Where are you when I need you to protect me? Can I come live in heaven with you? Are you mad at me, Lord? Do you hear me, Lord?"

I did not receive an answer, or so I thought, and I decided to take matters into my own hands. So, at the age of eleven, I took triple the directed amount of pain pills to kill myself, only to wake up the next morning. Angry, I tried to figure out why I was still there and the only thing that happened to me was that I got a good night's sleep. This was the third attempt on my life by the enemy—but God.

Since I felt like that the Lord would not let me take my own life, I decided that I would never let myself feel anything.

I taught myself not to feel the hurt and pain and not let others see it either. This was the beginning of me wearing a mask and putting up an invisible wall to shield me. I also learned to expect and prepare for bad, painful things to happen to me, never letting any situation or person get past my wall. I believed that this would allow me to get over hurtful things and people faster, that I would be able to survive.

Of course, there were times when things weren't as bad and I had fun with my siblings, but they were too far and few between. I always wished for those moments to last a little longer; but, knowing they would not, I looked forward to going to my mother. I was so excited when I knew it was time for her to pick me up. My bags at the door, I would eagerly look out the window for her car to pull up, but never without having hurtful comments hurled at me.

Not wanting to be prevented from going to my mother's, I no longer allowed the actions of my siblings to affect me or cause a reaction from me. My rally cry became "You must take it to survive" and "Never let anyone penetrate the wall." Seeing her car pull up, I'd quickly grab my things, and run out the door, ready to go to a better world that, like most things, was also about to change.

■

CHAPTER THREE

Where Do I Belong?

"But you belong to God, my dear children.
You have already won a victory over those people, because
the Spirit who lives in you is greater than the spirit who
lives in the world."

—1 John 4:4 (NLT)

Growing up with my mother always brought me joy. It was a place of refuge and love. I had almost every pet you could think of and was always involved in some type of activity; whatever I showed interest in, my mother made sure I at least tried it. I was involved in ballet, tap, jazz, bowling, and much more, always the tallest kid in my class. After being admitted into the adult dance classes as one of the youngest students, I found out I was great at dancing, loved to do it, and this was exciting. I remember my mother being so proud of me when she saw me performing and would say how talented I was.

When my mother got a divorce, it was just she and I for a while, and it seemed like the perfect world. We would do so much together and I felt special and safe. I had the biggest Christmas any little girl could dream of, and we celebrated birthdays and every holiday grandly. From dressing up and going to see the Easter Bunny and Santa to gathering with the neighborhood kids to set off fireworks, my mother did everything. As a young child, I never paid attention to whether or not I was treated differently from the other children in my mother's family—I just knew that I was being treated better than I was when I was with my birth mother.

My mother eventually found love and remarried when I was eight years old. I wanted my mother to be happy, but I felt like someone was coming in and taking my place and she would no longer want me. She reassured me that she would always love me and that he loved me as well. I cried for a long time, but, eventually, I saw that he did love me and took me in as his own. I thought to myself, "Wow, I now have a mom and dad!" and I was so excited! My father did have other children from a previous marriage and that was difficult at times. Just as I had seen him as taking my place, they saw me as taking theirs. For the most part, we got along when they came to visit or we went on family vacations; well, I got along with one of them and wasn't seen as a threat. It felt like the perfect life until, of course, it was time to go back to my birth mother's.

When I got a little older, my mother got pregnant. Those feelings of not being wanted resurfaced, but the excitement in the family was overwhelming. I was happy that I was going to have a younger sibling, but I couldn't help but wonder if my mother would still want or treat me the same. This was the only place I felt wanted. The heaviness of always wondering of your worth and permanence is tormenting for a child. While most kids have the security of going home to the same place every day and living with the same people, I did not. I was grateful, since, after all, my mother did not have to take me; she could have chosen any of my siblings. But, God had a plan for me.

The arrival of my sister was an exciting time that came with many changes. One was that my mother and father now had to care for an infant, and although they tried to make sure I was still able to do the things I enjoyed, having to tend to a baby took time away from me. When family would come to visit, they mainly came to see the baby and everything we did now had to involve either getting a sitter for my sister, taking her, or not going at all. I admit, this did bring a spirit of jealousy on me. In the beginning, I was not happy or very nice to her. Although she was just a baby, I felt threatened. We soon had to move and I had to leave my friends, which was sad for me. I was still going back and forth between my birth mother and my mother, but I was now even more upset because my sister got to stay with my mother and father all the time. Still going to two different churches and not able to attend the neighborhood school my friends attended, I wondered even more where I belonged.

I soon found myself with two sets of friends. My suburban friends were used to having nice clothing and doing things I would do with my mother. In my parents' neighborhood, we could ride bikes, play outside, go over to each other's homes, and even have sleepovers. We were all normally called to go in around the same time for dinner. Birthday party invites were a big deal, and at the end of the summer, we would talk about where we went on vacation. We never physically fought, since we knew that punishment would prevent us from seeing each other for a while. Besides, we were taught to work out our differences.

But my city friends in the DC public schools were different. Most of my siblings and friends did not get to ride a bike around the neighborhood because many didn't have one. Most of my friends in school lived in low-income housing and did not have much, which made it difficult sometimes for me to walk around with nice clothing. I often dealt with other girls not liking me because of the way I looked or carried myself, and they never bothered to get to know me. We never talked about summer vacations, because most never went anywhere. Hanging out at each other's homes was never the case either because there were always too many children in the home, which was never very well kept, or the parent mistrusted us with their belongings.

The one thing they did get to do that my suburban friends could not was to have a little more freedom. Now, this was kind of exciting and scary at the same time because we often roamed around, walking past drunks lying on the ground, drug dealers, and neighborhood kids trying to pick fights. Violence was a daily part of life in the areas my birth mother would move to. There were instances in which it hit close to home.

You can imagine how often I felt afraid over there. I was not a violent person nor did I like confrontation, but constantly being in that type of environment toughens you up. And, sometimes, it was difficult to shed one personality from another. If I had the personality I had with my suburban friends in the city, people took me as an easy target for bullying, and if I had the personality with my city friends in the suburban, people thought I was mean. It became harder and harder to decide who I truly was.

Although my jealousy for my baby sister left and I became protective of her, I was now old enough to notice that I was being treated differently from the other children in my mother's family by some of the adults. I'm not even sure if some of the adults were aware of the differences they were showing, but I received less money in my birthday cards, Christmas gifts were often less in value, and shows of love and affection were more sparse than for the other children. I'm not saying that they did not show or give me any love—just that there was a difference. There were times my sister and I would be together at functions or family reunions and family members would introduce my sister as my parents' daughter, often leaving me out or just saying, "And this is Yvette." There were times that I thought I was imagining this and became angry with myself because I felt like I was being ungrateful for what my mother had done for me. But, once I saw later in life that my own children had similar feelings, I know it wasn't my imagination.

The more I began to look around me and paid attention to the actions of those that were supposed to be family, I felt increasingly depressed and lonely. I would often watch my birth mother pour out the love I wanted onto some of my other siblings. My brothers were in and out of jail, and she would always be stressed out, looking for ways to get them out, visiting them no matter how far they were, attending family banquets that were held at the prisons. I watched how she would drop everything to be there for my sister (who was disrespectful to her), always making sure she availed herself to my sisters' children, treating our youngest sibling as if she was the prize gift. Knowing my siblings and cousins would always be able to feel and see that they had a family of their own made me feel left out and wanting the same.

But I dared not say anything to my birth mother nor did I say anything to my mother about how I felt. Of course, I did not want to hurt my mother or she think I was ungrateful, so I kept my feelings to myself and allowed the wall I put up to help me deal with the emotions. But as time went on, the mask started becoming a permanent fixture on my face. Thoughts of suicide were coming more often and my relationships with my natural siblings and birth mother were becoming more difficult to maintain. While attending middle school, my time was still divided between two different environments with two sets of friends. Like all kids, I had to keep my grades up, be active in school, and not do anything that would upset my birth mother or mother. In the teenage years, one discovers interests, begins to find love interests, figures out where one fits in at school; but I was still trying to figure out where I fit in at home.

I tried my best to make sure that my two worlds didn't know anything about each other. I made up stories to keep my suburban friends from knowing my mother was not my biological mother, or that I had other naturals siblings, and to keep my city friends from knowing that I didn't want to be in that environment, my aunt was the only mother I knew, or that I had another sister. I lied about my periodic disappearances, believing that, if I told them the truth, they would begin to ask questions I knew I would not want to answer.

Despite my efforts, there was always something done to remind me that I was never completely a part of either world. From my cousin spitefully telling mutual friends I was not my mother's biological child or one of my natural siblings or birth mother embarrassing me in public by yelling and stating that they were my "real" family, to my mother abruptly sending me back to my birth mother because she was angry about something I did—all of this forced me to accept that this was going to be my way of life and there was nothing I could do about it.

As I entered high school, I noticed my need to fit in and feel wanted and loved increased. But one good thing that happened was that I began living permanently with my mom and dad, not having to split my time by staying with my birth mother. Although I was still attending DC Public Schools and not the neighborhood school of my suburban friends, I was able to see them every day, hangout at the skating rink on Friday evenings and chatting on the phone for hours. Finally, I felt like I had some normalcy.

High school did bring a new set of challenges, especially since my mother was on staff at the high school I attended. This often caused me to become a target for bullying, especially amongst the students she would reprimand. Once again, without getting to know me, some girls would display jealousy, trying to provoke me into getting in some type of physical altercation and being just plain mean towards me; but I didn't let that stop me from trying to enjoy my high school experience. I became active in various clubs and captain of the majorettes, established some lifelong friends, got my driver's license and first car, started dating, and got my first job. I finally had what I thought was stability in my life.

Seeing as I was now free from the constant physical and verbal abuse of my birth mother, I wanted to try and have a healthy relationship with her and my natural siblings. To do so, I made sure I called to say hello, and I drove often to DC so that I might see and spend time with them, hoping my actions would show that I cared. I continued to try and make them happy and proud, becoming the first of my birth mother's children to graduate from high school. But none of my actions made much of a difference in our relationship: I would still receive harsh words and name-calling from my siblings, and my birth mother was too wrapped up in what was happening with everyone else to concern herself with me. This became more evident when I never received a phone call, card, or visit from any of them to see how I was doing after experiencing my first car accident, which was a serious one. My car was struck by a police cruiser that ran a red light with no emergency lights. Although the accident caused great damage to the vehicle, I was driving, yet my life was spared. This was the fourth attempt on my life by the enemy—But God

This incident had allowed me to come to terms and accept that I would never receive the kind of love a child would expect from the woman who gave birth to him or her. At the age of seventeen, having graduated from high school and now entering my freshman year in college, I rested in the security that at least my mother loved me and would never abandon me. That is until I did something that brought shame to my mother and father.

CHAPTER FOUR

Abandoned, Abused, and Living in Fear

"Have mercy on me, O God, have mercy! I look to you for protection. I will hide beneath the shadow of your wings until the danger passes by."

—Psalms 57:1(NLT)

My constant throwing up and light headiness prompted me to go to the doctors, only to receive the shocking news that I was expecting. Standing in the doctor's office, I tried to understand how that was possible since I was still having my menstrual cycle; I was then given even more shocking news that I was already three months pregnant. I walked around in a daze, wondering to myself what I, a sophomore in college, was going to do with a baby and how I was going to tell my mother.

This was going to be one of the scariest and most difficult things I would have to do. Thinking about how this would look to my mother's friends, family and church members, I knew she would be embarrassed about my situation, especially when image was important to our family. Even with these worries looming over me, I was happy at the thought of finally having someone who was mine, who was now a part of me, and I would love him or her so much and they would love me back. Feeling that no one could take him or her from me gave me comfort; even though I was not looking at the big picture and the responsibilities of becoming someone's mother, I just knew from the beginning that I would never abandon my child.

Bracing myself for the yelling, disappointed looks, multiple questions, and backlash, I finally gathering enough strength and asked her to come to my bedroom. Although I was trembling as I waited for her, deep down inside, I believed that everything was going to be okay and she would be there for me, helping me get through this scary period in my life. She would take me into her arms and be there to help me get through this pregnancy.

That was not the response I received. Instead, I received a stern look and was told, "Set up the appointment and let me know how much it will cost." I thought we had already moved onto prenatal care and was thinking, "Wow, she took this better than I thought." To make sure I understood correctly, I asked, "You want me to make a prenatal appointment?" Her response was not what I thought I would ever hear from my mother. She said firmly, "You will not have a baby in this house."

I was stunned by this ultimatum: Abort the child or find somewhere else to live. Out of everything that I had experienced in life up to that point, this was the most hurtful. My mind immediately wondered if she would give my sister the same choices had she gotten pregnant. How could she ask me to do such a thing?

Through my hurt and fears, I made the decision to keep my child. I was not going to abandon or kill my baby and, if my mother truly loved me, she would understand that. I also looked for my father to stand up and say something, tell my mother that an abortion was wrong in the eyes of Christ. Instead, he never said a word except about how I had disappointed my mother. Closing my bedroom door, I cried on my bed, asking the Lord if He was going to stand up for me, reminding Him that they taught us in church that abortion was wrong. I knew that having sex before marriage was wrong too, but I had repented—and now I had to kill my baby? Did no one see the hurt in my eyes? When would someone love, stand up, and fight for me?

Although I had nowhere to go, I began to pack my things. As I picked up the items in my bedroom, such as my TV, stereo system, and more, it was made clear to me by my mother that I could not take those things since they did not actually belong to me; those items were purchased by them. With tears in my eyes and in disbelief, I packed my clothes into trash bags and prepared to put them in my car. It was brand-new with air conditioning, one that I had worked and saved money to put down a substantial deposit on and only had for a few months. My first car that I got for my sixteenth birthday was a stick shift and did not have air, so I was proud of this accomplishment. But, as I was taking items out of the house, I was stopped at the door and asked to hand my father the car keys—I could not take the car since my father had co-signed for it. Later, that same car was given to my aunt without any of my deposit money being returned to me. Scared, confused, disappointed, hurt, and angry, I handed them the keys.

Gathering the rest of my things, I felt furious. Trying to figure out what to do next, I sat on my bed and began to replay everything in my mind. I looked for where I was wrong in feeling the way I did, but I could find nothing. Because I would not kill my baby, I was now being put out with my clothing in trash bags with no car, no money, nowhere to go. I never thought I would be here, being treated like this by my parents. After calling a friend to come pick me up and loading my trash bags full of clothes into her car, I went to say goodbye to my parents who never said anything back. I turned, walked out of the house, and closed the door behind me, leaving the people who I thought would never abandon me.

The drive to Howard University where my boyfriend, the father of my child, was staying was long and I could not stop crying. Thankfully, the Meridian Dorm was co-ed, so I was able to stay there for a short while as we figured out what the next steps would be. The only option I had at the time was to stay with him and his family in New York. Once the arraignments were made, I gathered my trash bags, caught a cab to the Greyhound bus station alone, and headed to Harlem. Terrified, sick, feeling alone, and abandoned, I was now placed in the care of his family whom I had only been around twice. Crying for days, I once again asked God: Why was I even born? I had been tossed like trash, first by my birth mother and now my mother; I became more and more angry than sad with my parents, especially my mother, because I knew she would never put my sister out and abandon her like she did me. I now didn't belong anywhere.

Soon, I was struggling to keep anything down and was feed intravenously so that I would not get to ill, going back and forth to the hospital to hold on to my baby. I was soon taken to an office to fill out paperwork for government assistance and Women, Infants, and Children (WIC) services, which I knew nothing about, and signed myself up with a pregnancy center just so I could have a support system. I'll always be thankful for his mother and siblings for being there for me, even though they were from another country and didn't know of Western remedies to aid my sickness. I had no one else and was simply doing whatever was necessary to survive.

God allowed me to meet a caring and kind woman at the pregnancy center I was registered with (because of her age she could have been my grandmother), who then took me under her wings and made sure I had all necessities. It was difficult at first for me to trust her or to let her get close to me since she was a stranger, and betrayal and hurt were all I had ever known up to this point in my life.

Knowing she lived on Riverside Drive, which was a very affluent area, I couldn't help but wonder what her motives were and why she wanted to help me. She seemed genuine and yet confused as to why I was in this predicament, often stating that I didn't look like I belonged there and asking where I was from and where my family was. Being one who hid behind the mask, I would shut down instead of responding to her. This did not deter her from doing nice things for me such as treating me to dinner, allowing me to spend time in her beautiful apartment, buying me maternity clothes, and going to my doctor appointments with me. After a while, I began to trust her and opening up a bit to her, but I was never willing to share too much about my past.

Looking back, I know that God placed her in my life during that season: She filled an empty void left by my mother. I often felt like I was dying, constantly in pain, going back and forth to the hospital due to dehydration, bleeding, blacking out from anemia, and going into pre-labor. I was unable to keep anything down which meant not getting enough nutrients for the baby or myself; I felt so alone. It was also during this time that I learned my difficulty in carrying children. I'd have to be on bed rest during most of my pregnancies, take medication to prevent early labor, and could not allow myself to be under any type of stress or I would have a miscarriage. Thanks to my efforts and the help I received, I was able to give birth to a beautiful little girl.

One evening, while at home recovering from the birth, I began feeling a pain like never before. Something hot gushed out of me and, when I looked down, I saw blood all over the floor. I called out for someone to help me. My boyfriend's mother came rushing in, yelling for someone to call 911; she then ran to gather up a bunch of bath towels for me to put in my pants to try and stop the bleeding. On the way to the hospital, I could feel myself getting weaker. Once arriving, they told me to sit in the waiting room. Everyone else was staring at me, wondering why no one was helping me. I heard someone yell, "Oh my God, someone help her!" I looked down and saw that blood was overflowing from the chair onto the floor, at which time I lost consciousness.

I awoke in a hospital bed with people around me concerned because my excessive loss of blood was the result of pieces of the placenta remaining in my uterus after giving birth. They were discussing whether or not to give me a blood transfusion, because the poison could have already started to spread throughout my bloodstream. Before I lost consciousness again, I asked the Lord if I was going to die. This was the fifth attempt of the enemy to take my life—but God.

The next time I woke up, I was not feeling the same. I asked the nurse if I was going to be okay and if they had given me a blood transfusion. Her response was no, I didn't need one because no poison was found in my blood, and I was going to be just fine, "Someone was watching over you," she said. Not soon after that, there were reports all over the news about people being infecting with HIV from receiving blood transfusion, since hospitals were not testing blood donations at the time—the hospital I was taken to was one such facility. I can look back and truly see the hand of God in my life.

Dealing with all of this and the feeling of abandonment, I wondered how I was going to care for a baby, go to school, and take care of myself. Should I try raising my daughter on my own as a student in college and single parent? Do I return to Washington D.C. with no job or place to stay? Do I leave my child with his mother to raise until I can get myself together, especially since my own family didn't want me? I had to make these serious decisions at eighteen and alone, and I entered a deep state of depression and felt more distant from God than I'd ever been. I decided that I would notify my mother to let her know I had given birth, hoping she wanted to meet my daughter.

I took the six-hour ride with my newborn daughter on a Greyhound bus to Washington, D.C. to see my mother, whom I hadn't seen or spoken too in almost eleven months. My stomach was in knots for most the trip. Somehow, I was able to fall asleep, only to be awakened to the bus driver announcing that we had arrived in Washington, D.C. Nervous and excited at the same time, I began preparing my daughter to meet her grandmother for the first time, making sure her clothing was perfect and her beautiful curls perfectly laying in place, then taking a second look at myself. Before exiting the bus, I paused to say a quick prayer—I hoped that, when my mother saw me, she would take me into her arms while telling me how sorry she was for putting me out and asking me to come back home. Unfortunately, this would be yet another prayer that would go unanswered.

As I exited the bus, it dawned on me how much I missed this place. I then grabbed my bags and headed inside the bus station to look for my mother. I spotted my mother in the distance and my little sister was standing beside her. Unable to see or speak with my little sister since leaving, I was more excited to see her than my mother. As my sister ran over to me with excitement in her eyes, she suddenly came to an abrupt stop, and looking confused, she asked me whose baby was I holding, which made me aware my mother never told her I was pregnant. Nervously, I stated that she was mine. With so much excitement, she began to jump up and down while saying, "I'm an auntie! Let me hold her." This filled my heart with joy, but I was still nervously waiting for my mother's reaction.

My mother gently asked how the ride was while reaching to peek and ultimately hold my baby.

While spending time with my parents and enjoying quality time with my little sister, I was faced with what to do next now that I was a mother. My boyfriend was no more ready to be a parent than I was and, he was still in school as well, which meant he was not in a financial position to care for our child or me. Although my visit with my parents went better than I expected, and my mother was helpful to me and my daughter, I was still not invited to come back home; so, with a heavy heart, I returned to New York with my baby.

Understanding that I needed help and didn't know anything about being a mother, I made the decision to ask my boyfriend's mom to help me with my daughter so that I could finish school and provide a stable life for her. She and my boyfriend's sister were there to help me with my daughter by helping to take care of her, potty-training her, showing me how to do her hair, and filling in the areas that I knew nothing about. They allowed me to concentrate on creating a more stable environment and ultimately becoming the best mother I could be. I am forever grateful for their help.

Although, my relationship with my own mother was being restored and she was helping me with my daughter more and more, we never discussed the ultimatum I was given when they found out I was pregnant. Because of this, my relationship with my parents changed dramatically. I accepted that I would never be treated equally to my sister. I was never angry or upset with my sister and remain protective of her to this day; she was just always treated better than me and I had to accept many things that would never be done to her. I concluded that I was in this world alone, and the only person who would always be there for me was myself.

While still carrying the hurt and disappointment from those memories, my relationship with my boyfriend began to take a turn, and because of his behavior, we broke up and got back together several times. Unfortunately, my need for love often sent me into whatever arms that extended themselves to me. Many ended up being bad relationships that included mental and physical abuse. When individuals know that you have insecurities, they will take advantage of that, and this is what happened to me. When you are young and thrown out to survive in a world you are not prepared for, you are taken to many dark places and forced to grow up fast.

After making the decision again to work things out and live with the father of my daughter, and eventually of our son, I went from pursuing my dreams to being in an abusive and controlling relationship. My boyfriend was a young man from Trinidad, Tobago, and although he moved here at the age of twelve, his views and behavior towards women were archaic and reflected many of the beliefs that I witnessed members of his family displaying. Knowing the relationship I had with my parents and knowing I had nowhere to escape to, he began to display dominating behavior towards me, which eventfully became worst. Turning from verbal abuse, and over time physical abuse, he controlled my money, kept track of my time, and monitored who I hung out with, trying to keep me from my friends and family.

I was always being accused of cheating, although he was doing the cheating. He would time me whenever I left to go anywhere, and if I didn't make it back in the timeframe he felt I should have, the verbal abuse would come. Since he was not willing to compromise with the car, I'd have to catch public transportation in rain, sleet, snow, and hail, while he drove everywhere. I was placed on a strict allowance, even though I was working a full-time job with the Federal government, and I had to ask for money even for feminine hygiene products or food. I had to pack lunches or go hungry, while he ate out almost every day.

I endured the frustration of having women in and out the apartments we shared—he always said it was something about "pursuing his music career"—but he was cheating on me. Being trapped and separated from family and friends and constantly being threatened, what was I to do? I had no one to run to. The verbal abuse then slowly started turning into a shove here and grab there, until one day, he hit me. Once again, I was at the mercy of someone who was supposed to care about me, but instead, he harmed me. For the second time, I attempted suicide, thinking it had to be better than being abuse again.

Growing up with verbal and physical abuse and then reliving it as an adult—it wasn't worth it to me. One night before bed, I took almost a half a bottle of sleeping pills. As I began to feel strange and feel the room spin, I gently laid my head on my pillow to let death take over. I had already prepared a suicide note, telling everyone how I felt. This was the sixth attempt on my life by the enemy— but God.

When I opened my eyes, I expected to see anything but my bedroom. Once again, I could not believe I did not die. At this point, I had pretty much given up on God or the hope that anyone would every truly love and care about me. My family often wondered why I would not just leave him, but where could I go? After all, they themselves had put me out, and I never wanted to be thrown out again, even if it meant that I would have to stay in this abusive relationship. If I was going to be made to feel less than, then I would just do it where I was. More and more, I began to rely on the barrier I placed up for emotional protection. I constantly reminded myself, "Yvette, if you do not let yourself feel any type of true love for this person and let them get to the core of your heart, you will survive this. Don't forget to wear your mask."

One spring day, we moved from Montgomery Country in Maryland to another apartment in Prince Georges County. I met this couple that was so sweet and kind to me, and I knew there was something different about them. I was right. When they saw us, they saw this young couple with two small children, the cutest family; if only they knew the horror and lone-liness behind the mask. When I would see them from time to time, they talked with me about Christ. At first, I did not want to hear what they had to say, because I still could not under-stand why God allowed me to be born into such jacked-up situations. Never wanting to let on that I knew much about Christ, I would avoid them at times, but I kept getting drawn back to them.

Then one day, I was stopped in the hallway of our apart-ment building and the woman told me, "God has a calling on your life. He's going to use you in a mighty way." Though I felt something strange going through my body, I just stood there. She then invited me to attend church with them and, before I could think, my mouth accepted. Not only did I start going to church with them, I was soon re-baptized. This was the begin-ning of me slowly allowing Christ back into my life, but I was still cautious. Funny how now I can look back and admit that I put myself in horrible situations, not Christ. He just allowed me free will.

The more and more I started going to church with them and going over to their home for bible study, the worst things seemed to get in my home. The accusations, verbal abuse, and physical altercations all increased. Desiring to be loved, I want-ed to run into another man's arms; after all, I was always being courted. It seems that not a day went by that another man was not offering to take me to lunch or dinner, or to give me something better in life than what I had. They constantly told me how I always looked sad and unhappy, and I was too beautiful to walk around that way. This was coming from both single and married men. Because I never allowed myself to have deep emotional connections in any of my relationships, I begin to entertain the thought of having someone better in my life. Not to mention that I was already angry, bitter, and vengeful for all the father of my children had done and was still doing to me.

Going to church and understanding the Word was good for me, but I still had not totally surrendered to Christ. I felt that no one knew what was best for me but me, and I was becoming stronger day by day to escape my situation. Paying more attention to the compliments paid to me and feeling a little better about myself, I was ready for a change. But I had a few things holding me back from running straight into another man's arms, or just leaving: First was fear of him harming me, and second was my two beautiful children, who were six and two. I could not leave them with their father and would never inflict them with the kind of pain I felt as a child, but how was I going to take them and provide for them, especially since I was told he would keep them from me and kill me before I left him? I ended up enduring the abuse for a little while longer, until that one faithful night.

While he was on his business trips, he would call several times a day, especially during those times he felt I should either be heading home, picking up the kids, or already home. If I did not answer the phone at the time or place he felt I should have been, he would scold and accuse me of doing any and everything, calling me a "slut," "hoe," and more. But one evening while he was away on business, I decided to go out after work, which was rare because I was always on a time restriction. So, when he called the house phone this particular night, I did not answer. When he returned from his business trip, things went downhill quickly. I got off from work, exhausted, and after picking up the children, I headed home to prepare my normal routine of helping with homework and making dinner. Instead, I walked into what seemed liked World War Three. I tried my best not to entertain what was happening because I was so tired of everything and was not happy he had returned home.

I prepared dinner to feed the children and settled them for the evening. As I was preparing myself for bed, I walked into our bedroom only to find the bed being stripped, and him pointing out stains on the bed, indicating that they were dried up semen from some man I was supposedly having sex with. He said he was going to put them in a plastic bag as evidence so he could get them tested. As I stood there in disbelief at what was being said, I responded, "Do you think that, if I had sex with another man in this bed, I would not have changed the sheets?" Then, he attacked.

I made up in my mind that, on this night, one of us was going to die and I was prepared to go to jail. Not realizing the amount of strength and anger I had in me, it went from him attacking me to me attacking him. After breaking away from him, running from the bedroom to the kitchen, I grabbed a butcher knife from the drawer, determined to hack it into his heart and watch him suffer and die. But instead, he fled from the home as I chased him out the front door. Once he was gone I knew this was my moment of escape. Realizing I had blood on me from a cut I received, I ran to clean myself up and gather what I could to run. I grabbed my children and made it out before he returned. Not sure if they would let me come but not having anywhere else to run to, I sought refuge at my parents. I entered their home, but not before I went into a full-blown asthma attack. This was the seventh attempt on my life by the enemy— but God.

I had finally escaped, moved into my own apartment with my two children and I was determined not to go back. It was time to pick up the pieces and put my life back together. But this was not going to be as easy as I thought. There were mornings I would leave to go to work and my tires would be slashed, or my car window broken and stereo system stolen. I never knew what to expect. From being stalked and my life being threatened, to going back and forth to court to get a protection order to fighting for custody of my children, every day I lived with the fear of not knowing where he was and what he was going to do. I fought every day. What I did know was that I was on my own again, ready to live life, all while hoping one day to find at least one decent person who would truly love me.

CHAPTER FIVE

Dating, Violated, and Near Death

"Though I walk in the midst of trouble, you preserve my life; you stretch out your hand against the wrath of my enemies, and your right hand delivers me."
—Psalms 138:7 (ESV)

Excited about my independence and freedom, I started dating. I was always attracted to older men and I admittedly had some shallow ways about me; for me to date a man, he had to be a certain height and have a certain look, all while being a gentleman. For a brief period, it seemed all the men I would meet were extremely attentive and generous with me; however, they also turned out to be married. Well, that was never going to work. I wanted my own husband to love and love me back. It also seemed as if there was some type of sign across my forehead that read, "Police officers only," because most of the men who approached me and showed interest in taking me out where cops.

While dating, I would make sure to remind myself to be extra cautious with my selection and to keep my wall up for emotional protection, not allowing anyone to penetrate it. I learned to care about people and even love them to an extent, but I would never give myself completely to anyone or be so in love with him that I was not able to walk away the moment I felt they were going to hurt me. And, after finding the strength to fight back in my abusive relationship, I promised myself that I would never allow another human being to put their hands on me again.

Starting to date, hanging out with friends, having fun: One would think life was good, but there was still a void and loneliness in my life. Yes, I did have my children, but this was a personal void; I was there providing and caring for them, but I had no one to do that for me. That is until an encounter I had one day in my high-rise apartment building.

Our eyes connected in the laundry room. I said to myself, "Wow, he's kind of a cute." Trying not to stare, I kept sneaking glances. Finally, he said hello to me, asking for my name and, of course, I was more than eager to tell him. After a brief conversation, we exchanged numbers. You see, I had just escaped an abusive relationship and my self-esteem was low; not only that but I was embarrassed about that relationship, feeling at times that it had been my fault that I had ignored so many warning signs. Many have asked why I had gone into that relationship in the first place, and my only response was, "When you've experienced some painful things growing up, it can cause you to do and accept things you never thought you would."

As we began to talk more and more, I learned that he was, again, a police officer. Not only was he cute, but he also had a god job and, based on conversations, seemed to be a nice man. Now during this time, I was struggling spiritually, still blaming God for the troubles of my life. I was slowly turning back to Him so I felt that I was rebuilding my relationship with Him, but I was not as committed to Him as He was to me and, because of that, I went off and did things that I knew wasn't pleasing to God. I was only trying to fill a void.

And that void led me to accept a date invitation from Mr. Fine Policeman. He invited me to go to a barbeque at his friend's house, so I was excited, especially because he wanted to take me around his friends. It was a beautiful summer day, the kind that's not too hot or humid. I was a little excited and yet nervous at the same time because this would be our first official date, and already liking him and believing he felt the same about me, I thought this was going to be a great day. Now, up to this point, we had never been intimate or even went out, and we spent our time just talking on the phone and in person, getting to know each other. I was excited about this as well, because I was so used to men immediately wanting to get physical with me.

I made sure I looked extra good for the barbeque. I put on my cute sundress and rocked my summer curls, ready to meet everyone. Little did I know that this was not your average summer date. After, meeting everyone and deciding to get a bite to eat, he offered to get me something to drink. Looking around at everyone, feeling cute and feeling good about my decision to attend with him, I had the biggest smile on my face. I thought to myself, "He's such a gentleman," as he handed me my drink and asked if I needed anything else.

He then gently reached to rub his hand down my face, telling me how beautiful I was. I immediately flinched thinking he was going to strike me. I was not comfortable yet with anyone putting their hands near my face. Confused, he sat beside me, sincerely wondering what was wrong. I softly told him that I was just cautious of anyone getting too close. I guess his training taught him to ask if I had ever been physically abused; I didn't want him to know my past at that moment, so I said no. He then told me that he would never hurt me.

As I sat there, listening to the various conversations around me, something strange began to happen to me. I went from "I feel so good" to becoming completely disoriented. "What's happening to me?" I asked myself. I began to see double and sometimes triple of people. I had never felt like this before; soon, I felt like I was going to die. "Please take me home," I told him.

I don't remember much of the ride home because I was going in and out of consciousness. I did become afraid and angry with myself for getting into this situation, and felt like something bad was about to happen to me. So, I began preparing myself to not feel anything, hoping my emotional wall would protect me. Although I was not in a committed relationship with Christ, He was the only one I knew to call on. He did not stop what happened to me, but He did keep me mostly conscious, allowing me to see and remember only key details. As the policeman raped me repeatedly, all I could do was repeat to myself, "Just take it. Don't feel. Take it to survive."

Calling on Jesus' name is what allowed me to not die that night from the drug he had given me or from him killing me to cover his tracks. After all, he was a police officer and knew what evidence they'd look for. In the blur, I could see that he kept going to the bathroom, flushing something down the toilet, which I learned later had to be the condoms he was using on me as to not leave his DNA in me. Still unable to move, I remained slightly conscious enough to see him walking around my bedroom to clean up, until he finally left and never came back. After that, I don't know how long I was unconscious for, but I woke to police officers surrounding me.

A friend of mine later came by and saw my front door slightly open, which they knew was strange. They found me in my bedroom unconscious, naked from my waist down, and called the police. As I began to regain consciousness, I could see the officers' mouths moving but I couldn't believe what I was hearing, thinking I was hallucinating from the date drug he had given me. I was hearing the two officers kneel beside me and pray over me. I thanked God for my life and for sending angels to pray over me, amid my disobedience and pain.

Later I learned that the two officers were Christians, saved and filled with the Holy Spirit. They also stated that I was calling on the name of Jesus as I was going in and out and, at that moment, they fell to their knees and began to pray and speak healing over me. After being rushed to the hospital, I went through the process of reporting a rape crime and felt re-violated. According to the doctor, I was given so much of the date drug that it was a miracle that I hadn't died from an overdose. This was the eighth attempt on my life by the enemy—but God.

While trying to recover and wrap my head around everything that had just happened to me, the situation became more complicated: The two officers who had prayed over me were no longer around, and the officers who took their place were now trying to make it seem as if this was not rape at all and I had drunkenly consented to sex. I understand the oath of protecting the "blue," but what about the oath of protecting the victim? They asked what *really* happened and if I was mad because I wanted more from the relationship and all he wanted was sex. I sat there, violated and insulted. Why were they accusing me of having had too much to drink, when I only had one *non-alcoholic* drink?

The officers told me how they were going to dig into my past and bring up everything that I did and drag my family into court if I pressed charges. Terrified that I would have to talk about what my brother did to me as a child, relieve the painful abuse I suffered growing up, or deal with my abusive ex, I was scared into not pressing charges. Instead, they had a stay-away order issued to the officer and made him move from the high rise we lived in.

At this point I was angry with myself because, as much as I wanted to get revenge on those who hurt me, something never allowed me to. What I did know was that I was done allowing men or anyone to hurt me first. From now on, it was going to be all about me and what I wanted, no matter who I would hurt along the way. From that point on, it was not others causing me harm, but me causing harm to myself from my reckless behavior.

I decided I would date and see whomever I wanted and didn't care who they were. If I wanted something, I went after it, making it perfectly clear to those I connected with that I did not want a serious relationship. For the first time in life, I thought only about me, aside from my two children. I went out, partied, drank, and dated. Because I was in pursuit of happiness for me, I never slept around with multiple people at one time and the places I frequented were mostly upscale social settings. I worked hard and made my way from the federal government to corporate America, making sure the individuals I was involved with were always well educated and professional. Some men could handle the non-committal relationship I wanted, and some couldn't. I endured more self-destruction, bad relationships, and hard-learned lessons.

The worst thing one can do is to walk around, not allowing oneself to feel the way human beings are meant to feel, but this was the only way I knew to survive. Many would find all this strange since I was so good at wearing a mask and pretending all was well with life, when instead, things were hard for me. While I was also trying to get my spiritual life right with Christ, once again the invisible sign "police officers only" must have been on display, because the one person who I decided to potentially have a serious relationship with turned out to be an officer. This relationship was one that propelled me to get myself together and to start getting closer to Christ.

CHAPTER SIX

∎

Deceived, Disobeyed, Forgiven, and Blessed

"If we confess our sins, he is faithful and just to forgive us our sins and to cleanse us from all unrighteousness."
—1 John 1:9 (ESV)

Here I go again: Entering a relationship and dating another police officer. Red flags were everywhere with this one, but did I pay attention to them? No. When would I learn? Things moved fast between us and, before I knew it, my two children, who were both in elementary school by now, and I were living with him, in the same neighborhood where my parents lived. Thinking we were going to have a life together, I settled into domestic life once again. I just didn't know it was going to be a short one.

Nothing about this relationship felt right from the beginning, and it was as if I was torturing myself for no reason, *again*. I was not physically attracted to this man nor was he a very nice person. Although something about him did not sit right with me, I continued down that road of deceit and belittling. Was it something that I had become so accustomed to that the abuse felt normal? Yes. My wall was still up, so I knew I would never have the kind of feelings I should have for someone I considered spending my life with. I also began to ask myself if I had a tendency to gravitate towards police officers because, in some kind of twisted way, I felt that they would protect me. Strange to think that, especially after being raped by one.

I went full steam ahead with this dysfunctional relationship. There was no physical abuse, but that ugly verbal abuse made itself at home—the kind that strips a person of her self-esteem and causes her to feel that *she* is lucky to have *him*, instead of the other way around. Fortunately, I was much stronger than before and didn't let anything he said tear me down.

It was also during this period that Christ started dealing with me more, and my visions and dreams came more frequently. I often knew things before they would happen or in places where I was not present. Not understanding what was happening to me, I did not share this with anyone for a while. I received prophecies about the relationship I was in, my life, and who I was in Christ. It seemed that, no matter where I went, the Lord was showing up and speaking to me more and more. While I'd sit in a visiting church or listen to a guest preacher at my church, the Lord would show up and use other men or women of God to speak over me; I'd always wonder how they knew so much about me when they didn't even know my name. It was uncomfortable, intriguing, embarrassing, encouraging, yet peaceful at the same time; somehow, I knew it was the Lord speaking to me and I felt a pull to something greater that I could not see or understand.

Mediating on those things spoken to me, my thoughts would travel back to my time in my great-grandparent's church. As a child, I saw men of God walk over to individuals and begin to speak over them, often telling them what God was about to do in their life. Some would look stunned, while others would weep. I'd sit there and stare, unable to move. My eyes would water up and my friends would want to know why I was crying; I would say, "It's not because I am sad. I feel something I cannot explain and it makes me cry." Of course, they would just say I was a crybaby, but my tears flowed because I felt something greater than anyone or anything that was present, and I felt safe. To this day, when in the presence of the Lord, I cry, not because of sadness, but humility, thankful that He loves me enough to allow me in His presence.

Soon, making a loving home yet while also living in sin became impossible. My boyfriend and I were living separate lives and, although he also had two children, we rarely did anything as a family; instead, I was dealing with constant disrespect, deceit, and lies. I understood that he was a police officer, which included working part-time jobs for extra money, but I soon sensed that the part-time jobs were a cover for other things. Still, I dealt with my unhappiness in the relationship because I did not want my children to have to leave their school, way of life, and friends; doing what I often did, I put others first. I was not emotionally attached to him anyway.

Although he constantly tried to make me feel insecure, delusional, less than, and unwanted, he never succeeded. I'd become a much stronger person and knew what he said were lies. There were times I would find women's undergarments and ask him who they belonged to, only for him to tell me that they were mine. Now, I do not know any woman who does not recognize her own undergarments, yet he would insist that I was crazy and that they were mine. Soon, I started receiving silent, hang-up calls on my phone or seeing the same car sitting across the street from my house, and I wondered if my children and I were being stalked. But like in my previous relationship, *he* constantly accused me of cheating and went as far as to have a recording device hidden and connected to our home phone, I grew weary of this relationship.

It did not help that, when my children and I went to church, I was told, "That is not the man God has for you." One Sunday service, a guest Bishop prophesied that God was calling me out of my darkness; there was a calling and an anointing on my life and, whatever I wanted to see, I only needed to ask God and he would show me. So, I started doing just that. Going before the Lord every day, I asked Him to show me what He wanted me to see, good or bad.

While sleeping one night, I awoke and jumped out of my bed yelling because I thought there were snakes in my bed, crawling all over me. Not understanding why the Lord showed me such a thing, I thought maybe I was not being clear enough with Him in my prayer requests. So, my prayers and questions started becoming more specific. I asked in detail about everything that was going on and for the Lord to reveal all so that no one could lie their way out or cause harm to me or my children. I was not prepared for what happen next.

One night while sleeping, a soft voice whispered in my ear, "You are sleeping with the enemy." I awoke and sat straight up and looked to my right. He was lying there sleeping, though I didn't recall when he got home or in the bed. This incident intrigued me, so I started showing up unannounced at one of his part-time jobs, which was at the mall. It was never planned, but occasionally, on my drive home from work, something would hit me and direct me to stop by there. Every time I did, I would find him with the same woman, either sitting somewhere eating or at the kiosk where she worked. He was even bold enough to introduce us as a way of deflecting suspension. She was married and had two children, and her husband was a D.C. Metropolitan police officer; I, being the cordial friendly person I am, held conversations with her whenever I would see her. But suspicion was always present when I'd come around and see the two of them together, even when it was her day off. Something never felt right in my spirit. He was always so cocky and arrogant, believing he had it all under control and things were going according to his plan—that is until one wild night.

There were times he would work at night, and when he did, I never heard from him until the next morning. He informed me that there were covert undercover drug cases, which meant that, if I tried to contact him on his cell phone, my calls would go unanswered. Since I understood this, I rarely called him or heard from him during the nights he worked, unless it was an emergency. So, on this particular weeknight, knowing he was working the night shift, I went on with my routine as usual, attending Bible study before returning home to settle in for the night. After putting the kids to bed, I went to relax and watch television while falling asleep; however, on this night, I kept getting an excessive amount of hang-up phone calls. Then, I would receive calls from him, asking me if everything was okay, which made that night seem even stranger. Unsure what was going on, I became restless and unable to fall asleep, so I'd just lay there and talked to God, reminding Him that, if there was anything I needed to see or know, He reveal it to me. After a while, the phone calls stopped, and I finally fell into a deep sleep.

The next day, my daughter called to inform me that the same car we had been noticing across the street from our house was out there again. Becoming nervous, I got ready to call my father to see if he would go down to the house to get the kids and make sure they were safe but, before I could, I received a phone call from a man I did not know. This unfamiliar voice identified himself as the husband of the woman sleeping with my man. He wanted to know if we could meet somewhere and talk. I'm not one to go off and meet strangers—I'm cautious and fearful of what might happen after my experience from being raped—but a soft, still voice in me kept telling me to meet him. So, with my guard on high alert, I arranged for us to meet in a public place. What happened next was something straight out of a television detective show.

This man proceeded to tell me how the car that my daughter and I had been seeing across the street was his. He had been videotaping the times I would leave with the kids for work and his wife would then come to our house, spending the day there. A light bulb went off—I now knew the source of the undergarments and other items that were left behind. He told me that, three nights ago, he told his wife he was scheduled to work a night shift, although he was not. He did this because he wanted to confirm what his son was trying to tell him: That a man would come to their house, take his mommy, and then bring her back.

So, three nights ago, while she thought he was working, he came home but did not park in their driveway. As he walked to his home, he noticed a parked van with movement in it, engine still running. Becoming suspicious, he quickly hurried to his front door to check on his family. The events he shared next with me left me sitting across from this man with my mouth wide open in disbelief.

Upon approaching his door, he realized it was unlocked and that his two children were in the home alone, his wife nowhere to be found. He ran from the house to the van across the street, which, at this point, was bouncing with movement. When he peeked inside, he noticed an individual who looked like his wife, so he began to try and open the door. As he did so, a man jumped into the driver's seat, put the van in gear, and sped off. He did not get a good look at the person, but from the description he gave me, I knew that it was indeed my man.

He then told me that he jumped into his car and proceeded to chase them down Route 301. Thinking they had lost him, the van looped back around, stopping in front of their home, where the wife jumped out to run inside, but not before her husband witnessed them. The van then sped off and, instead of chasing it, he stayed to confront his wife, who then confessed to everything.

Then, out of nowhere, this man pulled out a huge Ziploc bag with the negligee and panties she had on that night in the van. He wanted to give it to me as evidence to do whatever I wanted to with it. As strange as it seemed, I took the bag from him. Furious and feeling like a fool, I called my man to let him know I knew everything and I was coming for this woman, not to fight over a man, but to confront her for pretending in my face. The rage in me towards both of them was at a dangerous level. It's as if all the understanding, protection, kindness, concern, compassion, support, love, and forgiveness in me turned murderous. I jumped in my car and headed to the mall. While on my way, my phone kept ringing—it was my Bishop and his wife calling. I refused to answer because I did not want them to try and talk me down from my rage.

I pulled up in that mall parking lot on a mission, prepared to do bodily harm and go to jail if needed. No one had seen him, so I proceeded to the kiosk where she worked, bag in hand, ready to handle her; but she too was nowhere to be found, having called off for the evening. This only made me angrier because I knew he had warned her not to come to work and was too cowardly to show up himself. Feeling I needed to accomplish something, I handed her co-worker the bag with her undergarments and told her not only what was in the bag, but everything that happened. I knew she would spread the word.

Sitting in my car in the parking lot, I became even angrier because I could not do what I wanted. The phone kept ringing. Finally, with anger, I yelled at the top of my voice, "What do you want?" Then, I noticed that the Bishop and his wife had left a voicemail message. They told me they were praying for me and that the Lord showed them I was in danger. It wasn't danger from me getting harmed physically at that moment; it was the danger of me destroying so many lives around me, including my own. I wept in the parking lot. Even amid my fury, the Lord interceded on my behalf and protected me; my actions would have had detrimental consequences. This was the ninth time the enemy tried to take my life—but God.

After watching my man try to turn everything on me and then hearing every excuse possible, I realized I truly needed God. My children and I deserved more. What example was I setting for them? I just knew I could not and would not stay in an unhealthy relationship any longer. Once he was aware of this, he left: One day after returning home from a doctor's appointment, I opened my front door to find all the furniture gone except the kids' bedroom furniture and the bedroom set we shared. I was glad the relationship was over, but I now had to deal with the news I received from my doctor appointment: I was expecting.

I knew what I was carrying was a blessing despite my circumstances. Making my way to the altar, falling on my knees, I began to ask the Lord to forgive me. I did this every Sunday and before every Bible study. Then one day, while on my knees pregnant, something shot through my body and knocked me back. I begin to gag and liquid came pouring from my mouth.

The mothers in church shouted, "The Lord is purging her!" It was something I had no control over. As I continued lying at the altar, a lightness took over my body. It was as if I was floating, knowing I was on the floor at the altar and yet somehow I was looking down at myself. A white sheet suddenly covered me and I began to speak in a language I had never heard before. I began to weep. I remembered my childhood, my grandparent's church, and the very vision of the men and women being saved and filled with the Holy Spirit. That day had come for me.

CHAPTER SEVEN

Church Hurt, New Hope and Running from the Call

"A soft answer turns away wrath,
but a harsh word stirs up anger."
— **Proverbs 15:1 (ESV)**

God not only restored me, but also kept me covered even when I did not want covering. He even protected me from myself. I was now on a new journey, ready to leave all the difficulties from my past behind, with my eyes fixated on growing closer and stronger in Christ, all while making it through a difficult pregnancy. Although this journey brought its own set of challenges, I was in a much more serene space and place where I loved myself enough not to deal with anything that was going to bring me physical or spiritual harm. As I moved up in my career, saw my children growing up and doing well, fostering stronger relationships with my parents and sister. I felt more fulfilled than ever.

I gave God the glory and praise every opportunity I got, while becoming active in the Church and letting God use me as He saw fit. Many in the body of Christ, especially my spiritual parents, rejoiced for me because they knew my journey. However, there were some who were not pleased, feeling that a woman, pregnant, single, and with kids should not be used by God or serve in the church, and they made it known during "testimonies" in church meetings. While I may not have been the most knowledgeable person on the Word of God, I did know enough to recognize that what they said was not only wrong, it was not of God. One day, fed up with all the harsh and hurtful words that did nothing but bruise people's spirits, I boldly stood up.

The pastor had this nervous look as I stood up. So, I calmly started speaking, quoting 1 John 1:9, "If we confess our sins, he is faithful and just to forgive us our sins and to cleanse us from all unrighteousness." As some members began to clap and say "Amen," I asked this question: "Where in the scripture does it state that, for God to forgive and use someone to His glory, he needs to first get permission and acceptance from you?" There was silence first, and then suddenly, I heard laughter and someone yelled out "Hallelujah!" The pastor followed by saying, "Amen, Sister Yvette," and I breathed a sigh of relief. I continued going forth, becoming active in the church, despite the looks and comments I would receive from time to time. I told myself, they knew nothing about my life and from where God has brought me. What I did become aware of for the first time was that you can be bruised and hurt in the church.

It became another daily fight trying not to go into premature labor, especially having to work every day while tending to two other children alone. I was pregnant with a boy and my ex refused to be a part of the pregnancy or even help prepare for the child's arrival, but that did stop me from doing what was needed. I became so dependent on God that I trusted Him for everything, even if I could not see my way. One Sunday, while attending morning service, it was time for offering and, with my payday two days away, all I had to last me until then was five dollars. I knew I needed gas and did not have food at home, but I still walked to the front of the church and placed my money into the offering basket with joy. On the drive home, I did not know what I was going to feed my children or how I was going to get them to school and myself to work the next day.

Walking into our apartment, I headed straight to the kitchen, opening bare cabinets, hoping something was in there that I missed and could be prepared for dinner. Seeing that was not the case, I just stood there and said, "Lord, I need your help." A loud bang startled me from my daze; it was someone knocking at my door. Letting out a loud scream, I began to cry, worship, and praise God while standing in the doorway. My eyes could not believe what they were seeing: My spiritual parents were standing there with bags of groceries for me and the kids, telling me that, as they were leaving church, the Lord instructed them to go grocery shopping for me, for I had given my last in the offering. Not only did they fill my cupboards and refrigerator, they handed me an envelope that contained fifty dollars. I could not stop praising God, so they began to praise God with me. My faith and trust in the Lord strengthened that day—I knew that, no matter what came my way, I would be all right.

This faith was needed especially on those days I was too sick and weak to get out of bed, and my daughter had to see to it that her brother was ready for school. Driving them to school and myself to work were difficult tasks: I'd have to pull over several times because I would get so nauseous, and for those times when pulling over was impossible, I kept receptacles in the vehicle with me. Yes, there were times I laid in my bed and cried because, not only were my hormones all over the place, but because I was once again going through something so major alone. But this time, the Lord reminded me that I was not alone—I had Him, my family, and my church family.

My parents eventually became my greatest support system, often taking and picking up the children for me when I was not able, purchasing maternity clothes for me, preparing dinner for the kids and myself so that, after a long day of work, I did not have to go home and cook. They also gave me a beautiful baby shower and made things comfortable for me while I was on bed rest. Many days, I wondered what I was going to tell my son about his father when he was old enough. I was never one to bash or speak negatively about anyone, so I knew that when that moment came, I would just tell him the truth.

While my pregnancy took a toll on me, I grew closer and stronger in the Word, understanding more about the gifts God had given me, studying His word, and walking straight ahead into what I was being called to do, which was to encourage others and preach the Word of God. During this time, I reconnected with a gentleman who I had been friends with and had an on and off again relationship with for a few years. Unbelievably, he too was a police officer. Now, I made sure I was walking accordingly to God's Word, so all we would do was talk; I often shared my situation and a few other details from my life with him. Bothered and sadden, he wanted me to know that, if I needed anything, I could call him and he would be there for me. So, as the months went by and I got closer to my delivery day, we remained in constant contact, becoming the best of friends.

The month arrived for me to give birth and, although the father was not present, my parents and my sister were. It was a joyous blessing for me. I was so thankful to God for my daughter and now two sons, who were my world and I would do anything for them. Ready to move on and raise these beautiful children, I was hit with the unthinkable: I was served with papers to undergo a DNA test to determine if the boy was my ex's child. Although I was humiliated that my ex thought that I would be pregnant with someone else's child and angry that they had to stick my baby in his heel to draw blood, I went ahead and complied; I knew that, for the next eighteen years, he would be financially responsible for my son, and God had the rest.

Two years after giving birth to my son, I got married to my friend and love. We were ready to embrace new hope and a happier life, believing this relationship was right and that we were going to grow old together, especially because we had known each other for so long. I was also happy that he was there for not only my two-year-old son, becoming the only father he knew at that time, but also for my older children.

Continuing in my faithfulness to God, teaching Sunday school, leading praise and worship, ushering, and doing missionary work, I eventually accepted my calling into the ministry. Nervous, humbled, and yet excited, I studied God's Word and delivered my first sermon, becoming licensed as an Evangelist. Everyone rejoiced because they saw the labors that God had brought me through and how he loved me despite everything I had done.

But as I continued to allow God to use me, a spirit of fear came over me: The fear of not being good enough to preach the Word of God, fear of being judged by the saints, the fear of failing God. I often heard various people tell me how anointed I was and how that kind of anointing requires suffering, which made me start to think twice about preaching. The one thing I knew was that I had suffered enough in life and, if preaching God's Word was going to bring extra suffering, I did not want to preach. No, I was not giving up on God, but I no longer wanted to do what He was calling me to do. I decided that I would serve Him in other ways. So, I became even more active in women's ministries, choir, praise and worship, and traveling to various countries doing missions. What a bold, disobedient, and stupid thing to do.

While going on our second year of marriage, I discovered that I was expecting again. This would become my most difficult pregnancy yet, ultimately landing me on bed rest the entire time before welcoming another baby boy to the family. Feeling tremendously blessed and knowing that my children were the best things to ever happen in my life, I believed that the prayer I always longed for as a little girl had come true. These were my children whom I loved dearly and no one would take them for me.

Sadly, I brought old baggage with me into the marriage and my husband had some of his own. Though this marriage was not tumultuous, we were not equally yoked. We put our own eyes and feelings first, placing ourselves into situations that God had no intention for us to be in. Though I had realized that I no longer had to put a barrier up between Him and me, I still had one up in my personal life. It was not fair to my husband that, although I loved him, he would not have all of me, because there was still a part of me that I felt needed protecting. We had been friends for so long that our long conversations revealed a lot of things about each other, things I would never forgot. Some of those details were often pertaining to how one of us had betrayed another, so when I started seeing those traits in our marriage, I immediately became suspicious and shut down.

I often wondered if what I was going through was the result of me reaping what I had sowed in life, for all the hurt I had caused some individuals. Was this happening because there was no true stability in my life? Because I felt unwanted and abandoned, not knowing how to stay and work through conflicts? Was it because I always ran at the first sign of hurt?

When our marriage ended, we did everything possible to remain great co-parents so that our children would feel loved, although there were times it became challenging. Unlike my exes, he still cared and remained there for my son, seeing that he was the only father he knew; and for that I will forever be thankful. I could also see God creating peace between us, so that our children could remain children through the difficult process of separation and divorce. Still, I felt like a failure, wondering if I would ever stop running when hurt or pain came my way or if I would eventually stop running from my calling. I knew something had to change. I was now exhausted and ready to just surrender completely to Christ.

Transitioning from one relationship to another was something I never expected, especially so soon. I was not looking for a relationship, since I had decided I would remain single until God blessed me with someone who was best for me spiritually and not based on the shallow things I once required. I no longer wanted to make those decisions using my own judgment. For the first time, I was in a place in life where I wholeheartedly and truly wanted to live for the Lord and for myself. Believing I was healed from my past, I felt it was time to be more stable, more mature naturally and spiritually; I only wished I had been in the same place when my older children were younger.

Not wanting to look back at the many mistakes I made or all the pain I had endured in my past, I chose to focus instead on all that God was doing for my family and me. He was truly opening doors and blessing us. My two older children were getting ready to face the world, my daughter was finishing up her last year at Howard University, and my oldest son was about to graduate from high school and was headed for University of Maryland Eastern Shore. We were truly being blessed.

CHAPTER EIGHT

Love, Surrendering, and Broken

> *"When the righteous cry for help, the Lord hears and delivers them out of all their troubles. The Lord is near to the broken hearted and saves the crushed in spirit. Many are the afflictions of the righteous, but the Lord delivers him out of them all. He keeps all his bones; not one of them is broken."*
>
> — **Psalms 34 17-20 (ESV)**

While looking to further my education and seeking new employment, I received a call to come in for a job interview. Excited, I scheduled my interview date and prepared myself for a new beginning. Exiting the subway and heading to my potential workplace, I came upon what looked like a construction trailer. Standing there, I thought to myself, "This cannot be the place." But when I looked up, the name of the company was clearly displayed. Having worked in corporate America for the last ten years in nice office buildings with marble flooring and cherry wood desks, I could not believe I was standing in front of a construction trailer with my navy-blue suit and high heels. Once I got over the initial shock, I turned around to walk back to catch the train, all while saying to myself, "They must be crazy if they think I'm going to work in a trailer."

As I was riding down the escalator in disbelief and feeling like I had wasted my time and money coming down here, I heard that soft still voice whispering again in my ear, telling me to go back, because my blessing was there. Knowing it was the Lord's voice, I reluctantly turned around and went back for the interview; despite my resistance, I knew the Lord was blessing me financially, and that was a blessing I did not want to miss. Isaiah 55:8 tells us the Lord's thoughts and ways are not like our own, and His ways are beyond anything we can imagine; not only was this job a financial blessing, but it became something greater and more valuable.

When I met my current husband, I felt I had met the kindest, most respectful man I had come across in my life, and I knew there was something different about him. It was not his physical features that immediately caught my attention—I was always attracted to men who were at least six feet tall, since I was five feet eight inches, but this man was shorter than me without heels. Still, he was a genuine gentleman and, when I looked at him, I saw a big and hearty man.

Over time and daily conversations about anything from the news to the word of God, we developed a beautiful friendship. We both had a lot in common, both having come out of previous relationships that involved younger children, looking for a fresh start in life, and wanting to develop a stronger relationship with Christ. Our friendship eventually started growing into stronger feelings for one another and we wanted to spend more time together; so, we started dating. This was difficult for me since I was not looking to get into a relationship with anyone, and yet I began to have feelings for this man that I had never had for anyone else.

He made me want to share everything about my life with him, and for the first time, someone recognized that I was wearing a mask; thus, he asked me to remove it so he could get to know the real me. Slowly, I began to do something I promised myself never to do: To take off the mask and tear down the emotional barricade that I had up for so many years. Although fearful, exposed, and vulnerable, I continued. There was something different about this man that could not be explained. It was how he made me feel and not anything sexual. I was falling in love with his spirit, just from conversation and being in his presence. We would pray together and attend church services and Bible study, all while enjoying going to dinner, the movies, basketball games, and more. Since I always wanted someone who had their own personal relationship with Christ without my egging it on, I felt he was the one. Our connection developed and, I never wanted to do anything to cause him pain.

One night, while sleeping, I had a vision about him bound in chains, unable to break free, then a light appeared and the chains broke, and he transformed into this awesome man of God. Unsure as to what the dream meant at the time, I shared it with him, hoping he would have an answer; he did not. Still, that did not stop me from becoming more excited about where our relationship was going.

There were so many wonderful qualities in him that I also saw in my dad: They were a part of the same fraternity, active in the church, hard workers, and always respectable men. Although I knew people would question how fast our relationship was moving (mainly my family), I was in a place where I was no longer going to live and make decisions that would make everyone else happy. We both fully understood that we both were entering a relationship with previous baggage; however, this time was different for me. I had two handsome little boys that still needed to be raised, but I no longer had emotional baggage and was in a good place financially and spiritually; I made sure not to bring any drama or issues involving my ex into the relationship. I could not say the same for him.

Understandably, every relationship will have its problems, especially when you are dealing with blended families, but the amount of drama and issues that came with him was often too much for me to handle, especially considering everything I had overcome in my past. He did everything possible to shield me from it, but never had I dealt with being accused of so many things and my name being tarnished by individuals I had yet to meet. There were times I would end the relationship because it was too much to handle—I did not want any unnecessary drama around my children or me. But no breakup would last longer than a day; there was something calming about his spirit and the love I felt he truly had for me kept drawing me back.

Eventually, after two years of dating, he proposed and we married. Filled with joy and excitement, I knew I made the right decision and I looked forward to building a new life and growing closer to the Lord together. Although he had his own heartaches to deal with from a dysfunctional relationship in the past, he never allowed that to stop him from treating my children as his own. During this time, my husband received a temporary assignment, which lead us to relocate to Georgia temporary, so I left the workforce to stay with our children. This required me to be completely dependent on someone and that was scary for me, but I reassured myself through Psalms 37:25: "I have been young, and now am old, yet I have not seen the righteous forsaken or his children begging for bread."

I grew stronger and deeper in the Word of God, hungrier to do His will. I became more determined to surrender all of me to Him for His glory. While I was growing deeper in this spiritual relationship, my husband was finding his way as well. Moving again from Georgia to Virginia after his temporary assignment ended, our family became active immediately in the church we joined. My husband became a part of the men's choir and the audio team, and was appointed to the trustee board; our sons became part of the children's choir and junior ushers; and I became active in the women's ministry, women's choir, and liturgical dancers, while also teaching a class with my husband. We were a family that wanted to serve.

Life outside the church was good as well. Our children were active and doing well in school and various sports, my husband was moving up in his career and an active member in his fraternity alumni chapter. God had answered my prayers by surrounding me with amazing women who were more like sisters to me than friends. We were living in a beautiful home, able to travel to various places around the world, and expose our children to things in life many would never experience. Yet, I was still missing something. I was not living or fulfilling my purpose.

My husband was raised in a traditional Baptist church, so he was comfortable attending one; I, however, had attended a Pentecostal-Apostolic church, never forgetting my childhood experiences with my great-grandparents. I had to sit on my calling, since our Baptist Church did not recognize a ministerial license other than one obtained through the Baptist Association. However, this did not stop me from encouraging and praying for individuals, teaching, or being a witness for the Word of God. After all, a piece of paper was just a piece of paper, and I knew God had a greater purpose for my life.

Because my license would not be accepted or my gift acknowledged, I became unsure of what God wanted from me; therefore, I began to fast and pray before the Lord to look for answers. During my time of consecration, I reached for Proverbs 18:16 ("Giving a gift can open doors; it gives access to important people!"), Proverbs 3:5-6 ("Trust in the Lord with all your heart, and do not lean on your own understanding. In all your ways acknowledge him, and he will make straight your paths"), and Habakkuk 2:3 ("For still the vision awaits its appointed time; it hastens to the end—it will not lie. If it seems slow, wait for it; it will surely come; it will not delay"). I meditated on these scriptures. I was also reminded of a time two years before when I was instructed to start writing about my life. Each time I started, I was unable to finish since the pain would reappear as if it was happening at that moment. However, this time, I understood that the pain would always resurface so long as I did not allow complete healing to take place; so, out of obedience, I began writing my story and taking the time to heal completely. For a little over three years, I stood still and waited for God's appointed time for me to move in my purpose.

During my season of waiting, my faith, love for God and his people, revelation of His Word, commitment, dedication, and trust deepened; however, this season also rendered many challenges. I soon found myself slipping back into the old me, putting everyone's needs and feelings before mine, and I noticed my husband's treatment towards me was changing. He was going places and hanging out with individuals who were constantly cheating in their marriage, displaying behavior that was not becoming of a married man. He spent less time at home with the family, often only returning to lay his head down for a night's sleep before starting the next day. He also allowed others to disrespect me in his presence. I felt lonely. Our bond was obviously not as close as it had been, and communication often became difficult and disrespectful. I saw all the signs of hurt and trouble in our marriage, but I was determined not to run this time. I did not want to put my children through another separation and divorce.

I began to walk the floors of our home in prayer, asking the Lord to reveal what I needed to see and know about my marriage and my husband. I trusted in God, and prayed for Him to keep my husband from slipping away from Christ and me. Soon, my prayers shifted to being less about saving my marriage, but more about my husband's personal salvation. No matter the outcome, I was now rooted in God and would never run from Him again. For years, I continued being that virtuous wife, making sure my husband's reputation was protected, and no one knew about the disrespect, deceit, and un-faithfulness that was present in our marriage.

While going through all of this, our family was faced with two medical scares, two weddings, a horrific automobile accident, and a high school graduation; I made sure my children did not see any of the pain I was going through during this difficult time. Experiencing heavy and intense chest pains one day, I was rushed to the hospital. After many tests later, I was told that perhaps I had lupus or multiple sclerosis, but, in the end, they found out that I had mucus around my lungs, which was causing the pain. I was prescribed medication to take during flare ups for the next three years. Then, one Thursday evening while driving home from church after a bad storm, I was struck by a vehicle that ran a stop sign; the impact forced my truck to the opposite side of the street facing oncoming traffic. With all airbags deployed, my front window shattered, and smoke quickly filling up the truck, I tried to regain my composure, only to have an asthma attack. I was removed from the vehicle and transported to the hospital, where the doctor told me how lucky I was, because there were no broken bones, swelling on the brain, or internal damage. This was the tenth attempt on my life by the enemy—but God. I was so thankful that He spared my life, especially because my only daughter's wedding was just two weeks away.

I continued to pray for my husband and marriage, standing and waiting on God; then one weekend, I attended a Women in Ministry Retreat and God met me there. One beautiful day after having lunch, I decided to look out at the water and write a letter to God. When I got to the next session, a shift took place in the room, and God began to speak and move, using one of his prophetic messengers. Being sensitive to the spirit of God and knowing His voice, I begin to pray for His perfect will to be done, not expecting the shift to turn to me.

As the Lord began to use His vessel to speak to me, once again I was amazed, for only He knew what I had just written in my journal. At that moment, I heard the Lord say, "It's time. It's time to birth what has been deposited in you." Soon after, I began to experience pain like of childbirth and, unsure of what was going on, I looked down to make sure I was not about to give birth to another baby. Was I pregnant and did not know? I began to hear the Lord clearer, saying, "It is now time to walk in your purpose, to birth what has been deposited into you." On that day while lying on the floor, my ministry and purpose were birthed. Hallelujah!

Being filled with was so much joy and gratitude, I was now ready to see God move not only in my ministry, but also in my marriage; unfortunately, that would take another two years. I had to go through one more attempt on my life by the enemy: I started experiencing chest pains again, and the medication I was taking no longer worked, so I was referred to a cardiologist. I was then told that the previous diagnosis was incorrect and that they would have to look at my heart closer because of the possibility of a blockage. If there was one, they would do whatever was necessary to correct it. Doing the only thing I knew to do, I called on the name of Jesus.

I woke up from surgery to learn that my heart was fine and there was no blockage, just some fluid trapped between the heart and sack. They went on further to say how surprised they were that my heart was not damaged, because the fluid had been sitting in the sack for at least three years. Somehow, it had not become infected. This was the eleventh attempt on my life by the enemy—but God.

While still waiting for God to restore my marriage and my husband, I stayed in prayer, telling the Lord this battle was now his and I could no longer fight it. I was still being obedient to the Lord, fulfilling any ministerial assignments given, and remaining a faithful wife and dedicated mother, but I was becoming broken from all the hurt and pain. I was no longer willing to protect my husband's reputation or deal with his disrespectful behavior. With the storms raging in my life, I put all my trust in God even though the things I saw through my natural eyes were telling me not to believe; I began to praise and worship Him like I was losing my mind. Determined to get my breakthrough, I declared to the enemy and began to speak with authority: "I am sick and tired of your games. I will wait on the move of God even though I'm in this holding place. No matter what it looks like, no weapon formed against me and my family will prosper." I surrounded myself only with women of God who interceded and spoke words of encouragement into my life. Walking around anointing my home, praying in every room and lying prostrate before the Lord, I prayed for my husband until God told me to move.

One day, I heard the Lord speaking to me in that soft still voice saying, "It's not over, until I say it's over. It's time." I then confronted my husband, revealing to him everything I knew and reminding him of the relationship he once had with Christ. I showed him how he had allowed the enemy to pull him in the wrong direction, and walk away from God and his family; I told him I was not going backwards but instead moving forward. He now had a decision to make.

Looking in to my husband's eyes, I could see the look of disbelief because of the things I knew. Also, he wore the look of embarrassment, shame, and hurt he was feeling for what he put our family through, especially me. As my husband was going through his own period of brokenness, God began to humble him, removing the scales from his eyes, allowing him to see things clearer. He began to recognize he had some generational curses on him and had been displaying the same behavior he once witnessed. My husband began repenting and surrendering to God. Afterwards, he looked at me and said, "I love you. Please forgive me. I don't want to lose my wife and family. I will do whatever is necessary to repair our marriage and family."

My love for God, His Holy Word, and my love for my husband allowed me to forgive him. Luke 17:4 states, "And if he sins against you seven times in the day, and turns to you seven times, saying, 'I repent,' you must forgive him."

It was now time for my complete restoration and healing.

CHAPTER NINE

Healing and Restoration

"For I will restore health to you, and your wounds I will heal, declares the Lord, because they have called you an outcast: 'It is Zion, for whom no one cares!'"

— **Jeremiah 30:17**

God was beginning to heal my marriage and my family, and now He was healing me completely. As I lay on my bedroom floor, allowing God to have his way with me, I began to cry out and confess how deeply I needed Him. Realizing I need Him like the desert needs the rain and the morning needs the sun, I now knew that I couldn't breathe or live without Him in my life. He was the only one who never left me. I began to get my breakthrough and rise out of my situation, problems, depression, heartache, fear, worrying, circumstances, disappointments, troubles, past mistakes, and tribulations.

God turned me away from negativity and my past and, instead, urged me to view my life through His eyes. I began to see that everything I went through was for a greater outcome, and I was being prepared for the anointing and assignments He was placing on my life. Looking with compassionate eyes, I soon understood that it must have been hard for my siblings to grow up in an environment where there was no escape for them; they had to watch me live a life they wish they had. What made me so special? He also allowed me to see that my birth mother was very young and had been raised in a strict Christian family, so she had no choice but to get married when she found out she was pregnant with her oldest child; she was still just a child herself and a survivor of domestic abuse. I was then able to see how challenging it must have been for my mother, taking a child of a family member and then going through a divorce, only to have all these stipulations in place to continue having a relationship with that child. Not once did she say, "I do not want to or have to deal with this."

While lying prostrate before the Lord, I began to feel peace come over me, and from nowhere came a laughter that I was unable to control—it was the Lord filling me with His joy and neither my heart nor my body were aching anymore. Getting up on to my knees, I worshiped and praised God like never before and then began to shout around my room because my greater was here. My deliverance, healing, and breakthrough were here, and I was now walking into a new season; I was walking into my destiny. God had healed me and given me the vision of my husband being freed from shackles before turning into a righteous man of God. It was manifesting before my eyes. My husband became thirsty and hungrier for the Word of God, and his walk and relationship were restored—a spirit of peace had come over him.

God allowed us to receive spiritual counseling during this time and, when we were not in counseling, we sat and talked for hours about everything. We begin to study biblical reading plans together while enjoying each other's company. My husband changed the company he was keeping, recognizing that their lifestyles did not line up with the Word of God, and he constantly made sure that the conversations he was having were never disrespectful to his wife.

Mathew 19:6 states, "So, they are no longer two but one flesh. What therefore God has joined together, let not man separate" (ESV). When we look in to each other's eyes now, there is a renewed love that we have for each other, a closeness we never had before. There is joy, laughter, and peace in our home, and we are walking side by side as one, determined to fulfill all God has called us to do. Looking at me, my husband says, "Thank you for not giving up on me."

I am now walking with a new joy and am no longer bound by the hidden things in my past. My hurt and disappointment are long gone, and have been replaced with compassion and forgiveness.

EPILOGUE

My Purpose

"And he gave the apostles, the prophets, the evangelists, the shepherds and teachers, to equip the saints for the work of ministry, for building up the body of Christ."
— **Psalm 18:6 (NLT)**

As the Lord began to reveal my purpose, He also unveiled my calling, an anointing and favor on my life. But just because one has favor does not mean she or he does not have hurt or will not go through tribulations. I had to understand that, until I whipped the things that are right in front of me, I was not eligible nor equipped to whip the things that God was about to do in my life. Until I learned to have a relationship with those in my house and to not suppress everything, how could I have a relationship with the people He would assign to me? God gives me conflict so that I can learn to bring resolution—if I cannot bring about resolution in a small area of my life, why would the Lord trust me with something big?

He showed me that the anointing comes with a price. The price of separation, trials, heartache, betrayals, disappointments, and brokenness all help to build, strengthen, and mold me in the spirit so that the birthing of humility, compassion, steadfastness, commitment, boldness, and fearlessness could come forth. My past does not define me, and I was carefully and meticulously created to be all that God has ordained me to be and to walk in my Kingdom Authority: "I praise you because I am fearfully and wonderfully made; your works are wonderful; I know that full well (Psalm 18:6 NLT).

Now, I take and use all of this to encourage, empower, and minister the unadulterated true Word of God to His people. My purpose is to be that walking testimony, an encourager, prayer warrior, and witness to others. I was once that vessel that had been stained, yet God cleansed me to be used for His glory, and from that birthing came "Just A Diva Encouraging Ministries." Diva generally has a negative connotation attached to it, but here, it stands for Divine, Inspiring, Virtuous, and Anointed (DIVA). Our primary mission is to encourage the discouraged, all while helping the people to unmask themselves and be set free from the things that are holding them in bondage.

I now stand in the gap and intercede for those who have attempted or contemplated suicide; to have compassion, minister to and encourage those who feel like they do not belong, fit in, or have a purpose; to lend a hand to those who have been molested, raped, abused, abandoned, divorced, neglected, or are afraid. I remind them that there is a God who loves them and has given His life for them, so all they must do is hold on to God's unchanging hand. He will never leave you or forsake you, and he can take your pain and turn it into your purpose. He is on your side and will do just what He said.

So, as God continues to take the limits off me and enlarge my territory, I will continue walking in my kingdom authority, encouraging all He sends my way. I am a survivor, an overcomer, a living walking testimony that is walking in her deliverance, breakthrough, healing, prosperity, calling, gift, protection, healing, promise, and anointing. And everything God calls me to do, I shall do: "I have been crucified with Christ. It is no longer I who live, but Christ who lives in me. And the life I now live in the flesh I live by faith in the Son of God, who loved me and gave himself for me." (Galatians 2:20)

For my pain had purpose.

About the Author

Evangelist Yvette Steele is an author, minister, mother, grand-mother, and woman of God. She received her Evangelist license to preach from the Ministry of Love Apostolic Church. She is the founder of JADE Ministries and Just **A** Diva (**D**ivine, **I**nspiring, **V**irtuous, **A**nointed) **E**ncouraging Ministries, and the creator of JADE's BLOG. She is also an active and leading member of her church, and a philanthropist and missionary who has traveled to Jamaica, Haiti, and the Dominican Republic to perform mission work. In 2015, she received the Metro Phenomenal Woman Award from the Millennium Business Advisors for her efforts and achievements. She is currently furthering her education seeking a degree in theology from the Regent University of Theology.

Steele resides in Chantilly, Virginia, with her husband and two of their four children. When she is not encouraging the discouraged to walk in their Kingdom Authority, she enjoys reading, swimming, biking, doing Zumba, and traveling.

CREATING DISTINCTIVE BOOKS
WITH INTENTIONAL RESULTS

We're a collaborative group of creative masterminds
with a mission to produce high-quality books to position
you for monumental success in the marketplace.

Our professional team of writers, editors, designers,
and marketing strategists work closely together to ensure
that every detail of your book is a clear representation
of the message in your writing.

Want to know more?
Write to us at info@publishyourgift.com
or call (888) 949-6228

Discover great books, exclusive offers, and more at
www.PublishYourGift.com

Connect with us on social media

@publishyourgift

CPSIA information can be obtained
at www.ICGtesting.com
Printed in the USA
FSOW04n2354230717
36490FS